gör lite vad du vill
men se för fan till att
FÖRSÖRJA dig
FÖRÄNDRA dig
FÖRVERKLIGA dig
och var jävligt snygg
och normal under tiden
så löser nog det här sig
ska du se.

Quote from the book, "Everything will be Alright," by Lisa Ewald (Galago 2013). See overleaf for English translation.

Freestyle embroidery on wool

How to create your own embroidered wool appliqué designs

Karin Derland

Photography by Jenny Unnegård

Pimpernel Press Ltd
www.pimpernelpress.com

For Grandmother
– for all the moments. You have always seen.

Do a little of what you want
But make sure that you
Take care of yourself
Change
Get real
And be super nice
And usually, over time,
You will see a solution

(English translation of photo opposite title page)

Freestyle Embroidery on Wool
First published in Sweden in 2018 as *Brodera fritt på ylle* by
The Swedish Handicraft Publisher and The National Association of Swedish Handicraft Societies (SHR)
www.hemslojdensforlag.se
This edition published by Pimpernel Press Ltd in 2020

Photography: Jenny Unnegård
Instructions, illustrations, and text: Karin Derland
Translation into English by Carol Huebscher Rhoades
Editor: Cecilia Lungström
Design: Cecilia Ljungström
Publisher: Ulrika Rapp

A catalogue record for this book is available from the British Library.
ISBN 978-1-91025829-3
Typeset in Adobe Caslon and Utopia
Printed and bound in China by C&C Offset Printing Company Limited

10 9 8 7 6 5 4 3 2 1

Contents

Introduction

Sometimes I realize that embroidery, in contrast to painting or other artistic forms of expression, is often limited by rules and views about how one should work, particularly regarding technique. The picture of a lecturing craftswoman looms into view when you mention that you embroider. Surprisingly, quite a few people have preconceived notions and associate the craft primarily with stiff, boring handwork and flowery vines.

Personally, I see embroidery as a way of expressing myself, as I would with any other artistic medium. It is also a convenient means for exploring and experimenting with textile materials and techniques.

This is not a traditional how-to book for wool appliqué embroidery with set patterns and exact descriptions. Instead I want to share my thoughts concerning form, inspiration, materials, techniques, and composition. I have found a way to embroider that is ever-changing and seldom predictable. The intention is not for you to replicate what I have done. It is impossible to explain in words the creative process that I go through to achieve my work. That belongs to the inner world – that which makes us all unique spirits.

I am often told that my work is recognizable by its symmetry and balance. It encompasses many factors. I've always felt a restlessness within me and a strong need to visualize in order to find structure. Embroidery by its nature forces me to slow down and, at the same time, to channel the myriad ideas within. In essence: inside moving – outside structure = some form of balance…

Skip planning in detail

When I embroider I may have vague thoughts and ideas about the final result but I never decide ahead of time how the embroidery should look in detail. Partly because it might kill all the creativity and partly because I cannot work that way as it doesn't allow for ideas arising as I go along. When I work with an embroidery, I make many choices along the way. For me, composition, color, materials and stitch choices are largely connected with thoughts, associations, and insights that occur in the moment and during the process. The risk in trying to plan ahead and organize how everything should look is that I latch on to a thousand decisions about details with the result that it doesn't become anything. For me, embroidery is an ongoing creative process that has little to do with the mechanical completion of something already decided in detail ahead of time.

When I embroider, I'm always shifting between techniques and materials. The outlines of appliqués are blended with illustrations freely drawn directly on the fabric. The various types of stitches worked directly on the background fabric are interwoven with stitches on the appliquéd fabric. Besides the threads, beads, mirrors, sequins, ribbons, metal threads, and much more are all used. There are few pointers (and yes, it works just fine to knot the thread at the start). This book covers some of the practical aspects such as different materials and how you can compose your own patterns with the help of your own templates, but most of all, it is about how you can think about inspiration, color, form and composition. The starting points in my own work are shown as examples and to demonstrate the impact of assorted details. For those who still feel a need for a couple of hand-holding, step-by-step projects, before you set off on your own, the book ends with a few projects.

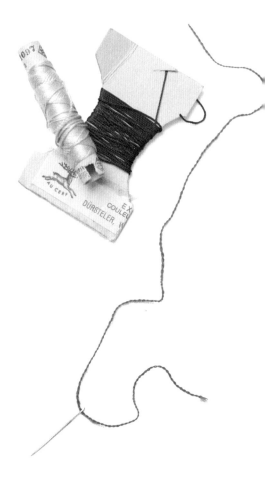

Choose your own level of difficulty

I do not have any traditional training in the art of sewing, I have never taken a course in embroidery. I am self-taught, have experimented, and learned by experience. Different art school studies in drawing, painting, sculpture, and graphics as well as working on newspaper layout – work highly focused on symmetry and balance, empty space versus filled areas – have very clearly trained my eye and influenced the way I compose my work.

THE INTENTION IS NOT THAT YOU REPLICATE WHAT I HAVE DONE. IT IS IMPOSSIBLE TO EXPLAIN IN WORDS THE CREATIVE PROCESS THAT I GO THROUGH.

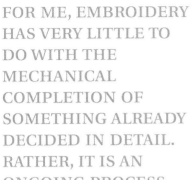

FOR ME, EMBROIDERY HAS VERY LITTLE TO DO WITH THE MECHANICAL COMPLETION OF SOMETHING ALREADY DECIDED IN DETAIL. RATHER, IT IS AN ONGOING PROCESS.

Choose the techniques and level of difficulty to suit yourself. Finally, either keep to a simple composition with basic stitches, a limited number of threads, fabrics, and shapes, or immerse yourself in a large assortment of details, materials, and more advanced stitch techniques. It will be something, no matter which path you choose and how much experience you have.

Choose your preferred level of difficulty – begin with the stitch techniques and materials that appeal to you.

BEFORE
YOU BEGIN

Tools and materials, inspiration, and templates;

composing patterns and thinking a bit about

color choices.

Tools

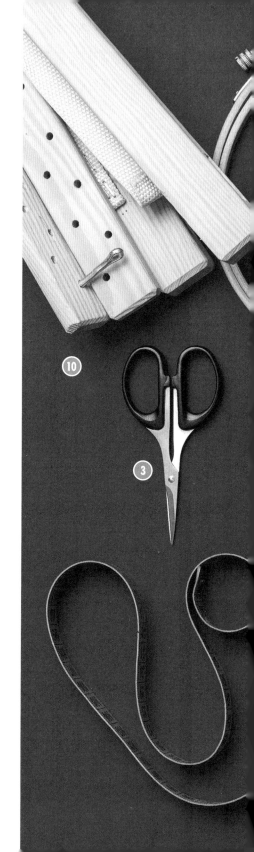

Besides needles and scissors, a number of other tools simplify embroidering on wool with appliqué techniques.

1. **Needles with sharp tips** in various sizes (no. 18, 20, and 22 are a good basic assortment plus a few very fine sewing and bead needles if you want to embroider on small beads and sequins. Most important is choosing needles large enough for the fabric and thread you are using. The needle, not the yarn, makes the holes in the fabric. Does the needle drag as it goes through the fabric? Change needle size!

2. **Larger size fabric scissors,** for cutting out the background fabric and larger pieces of appliqué.

3. **Small embroidery scissors,** for cutting thread and small appliqué details and for unpicking if necessary.

4. **Paper scissors,** for cutting out templates.

5. **Small ruler,** about 6in/15cm long. Very handy for measuring small items.

6. **Lead pencil,** for sketching, drawing templates, and marking on light fabric.

7. **White gel pen,** for marking on dark fabric.

8. **Measuring tape,** for measuring fabric and larger items.

9. **Embroidery hoop,** good to have if you tend to tighten the stitches a lot. Generally necessary if you embroider couching.

10. **Large embroidery frame/stretcher,** good if you want to keep the entire embroidery taut as you sew.

11. **Graph or unlined paper,** to sketch shapes, patterns, etc.

12. **Cardstock,** for making templates.

13. **Plastic stencil,** if you want to transfer pattern details to fabric.

14. **Black water-resistant marking pen,** to trace patterns onto a plastic template.

15. **Beeswax,** drag thread over a bit of wax to make a frayed linen thread smoother and stronger.

Materials

Fabric

Kläde and *wadmal* are types of 100% wool fabrics. They are made from woven fabric that is fulled (a process similar to felting), trimmed and pressed until they have a smooth and even surface. These fabrics are especially good for embroidery. Both variations can be found in a variety of qualities, thicknesses, and manufacture and it can be difficult to distinguish between them. Historically, kläde was an exclusive fabric: thin, supple, made with the finest wool, and excellent for elegant clothing. Wadmal was a heavy fabric that was fulled so hard that the individual threads could not be distinguished. Nowadays, the line between wadmal and kläde has loosened but the names live on to designate finer and heavier fulled wool fabric. I almost exclusively use finer wadmal. Whichever you choose, look for a good quality that won't fray when you cut out the appliqués.

I urge you to refrain from using the so-called hobby felt. It is sold in craft stores and might resemble wool fabric because it sometimes contains a small amount of wool. But hobby felt is not nearly as durable and pliant and there is a risk that your finished embroidery – on which you've spent a lot of time working – will lose its shape, acquire noils, and look shoddy. I also avoid wool felt with polyester blended in for those reasons. You will find both small and large pieces of real wadmal/kläde in Swedish and Norwegian handicraft stores, embroidery shops, and well-stocked fabric stores (see page 135). Some pure new wool furniture fabrics serve well for embroidery – try it out yourself.

> **TIP**
>
> *You can combine kläde and wadmal of different thickness and quality in the same piece.*

Other advantages with wadmal/kläde are that they are smooth (no holes from the weave or other notable structural elements to cause problems), flexible, and pretty. Wool also repels dirt. Older wool embroideries can look clean and fine despite their age and any flecks are usually easy to brush away with a little lukewarm water. Dust and hair strands can be removed with a lint roller.

Embroidery thread

Which thread to embroider with is an individual choice – wool, linen, silk, regular matt or mercerized (more lustrous) cotton, to name a few – most work well. Personally, I always blend different types, that is to say, I never embroider only with wool or only with linen but alternate various sections and stitches with different yarns because their characteristics and looks shift.

Embroidery thread is sold either in hanks or in skeins. A skein is basically a small hank. Some yarns are multi-ply and can be separated so that you can sew with one or two strands.

Beads, mirrors, ribbon, and embellishments

Besides yarn, you can use a whole assortment of items to good effect when you embroider. Beads, sequins, mirror mosaics, even finished appliqués with, for example, rhinestones and decorative ribbons of different types add another dimension to the embroidery. It is fun to experiment with a variety of materials and also the end result will be more exciting and dynamic. You'll find all kinds of materials to use for embroidery in hobby, fabric, and sewing shops.

Of course, it is a question of balance about how much you want to use for what – it might not be very comfortable to rest your head on a pillow full of beads and sequins. You also have to consider the possibility of breakage. But, on a wall-hanging or picture, it doesn't matter. Furthermore, some small beads sewn on with doubled strong thread can work well even on a pillow.

SOME GOOD THREADS

→

WHICH NEEDLE?

It is very important that the needle be sufficiently large for the fabric and yarn as needed – it is the needle, not the yarn, that makes the holes in fabric. Does the needle drag as it goes through? Change needle size!

TIP

For borders and edgings in laid work, you can even use cords, braids, or string. There are also metallic colored threads that can be very pretty.

Tapestry wool ①

Tapestry wool is a thick, fluffy wool yarn that fills in well. It can even be separated. Many colors and brands are sold in skeins in well-stocked yarn stores.

Mora redgarn ②

Mora redgarn (20/2) is a very fine and soft wool yarn with a firm twist that prevents it from breaking easily. Available in many colors. If you want to use it for denser filling, combine strands together. Buy in hanks or smaller skeins at handcraft shops (www.borgsvavgarner.se).

Brage yarn ③

One of my favorite yarns, Brage (7.5/2) yarn is a coarse, rather stiff and firmly-plied wool yarn. It works well for many different types of stitches – from double-sided long-and-short stitches to stem stitch. Available in many colors. Buy in the hank or in smaller skeins at craft shops (www.borgsvavgarner.se).

Tuna yarn ④

Tuna (6/2) is a wool yarn that is softer and not as firmly plied as Brage. It is available in many colors and shades. Buy in skeins or small hanks at handicraft shops (www.borgsvavgarner.se).

Linen yarn ⑤

Linen yarn is stiffer and less flexible than cotton, but is very fine on wool fabric. Available in many colors and brands and sold in hanks. The amount of luster depends on the brand. I use linen quite a lot and for many different types of stitches. It comes in a variety of sizes but 16/2 is a good option.

Lace yarn ⑥

Lace yarn is a linen yarn available in a variety of sizes. It is very durable even when quite fine. It is good for sewing on very small appliqués, beads, and sequins. It is even good for finishing.

Silk ⑦

Silk is smooth, more expensive, and sometimes a little more difficult to find. It is unbelievably beautiful against a matt wool fabric and fantastic to embroider with – a good choice for details. Comes in various sizes and qualities.

Pearl Cotton ⑧

Pearl cotton is a firmly plied and mercerized (shiny) cotton thread. Its luster shines prettily against wool fabric. Comes in many different sizes and colors. Sizes 3/2 and 5/2 are heavier while 12/2 is finer. Works as both a filler and for lines.

Mouliné ⑨

Mouliné is a mercerized (lustrous) loosely plied cotton thread that is easy to separate if you want thinner pieces. I seldom use it because I prefer a more firmly plied thread but I am listing it because it is one many stitchers are familiar with and it's easy to find at yarn and craft shops. You can buy it in skeins and in many, many colors!

String ⑩

String is a loosely plied cotton thread used to make heavier string. Can be used as edging with laid work. Primarily considered as weft for weaving.

See photo overleaf

SUGGESTIONS FOR BEADS, MIRRORS, AND RIBBON

Rocaille beads ❶

Rocaille beads are small beads, usually glass. They come in a large variety of colors, sizes, and variants – everything from matt single-color to striped and metallic. Look for them in hobby and sewing shops or specialty bead shops. Rocaille beads are good because they are small and blend in well, but, of course, you can use whatever beads you like. Either string them onto the thread you are embroidering with, if the bead holes and the thread match each other, or sew them directly onto the fabric with fine thread.

Wood beads ❷

Wood beads come in many sizes, colors and designs. They provide a rustic look and, for example, are good for garlands.

Sequins ❸

Sequins can be found in many shapes, colors and sizes in hobby or sewing shops.

Jewelry components ❹

You can find large assortments and varieties of pieces for jewelry making in shops. Many are excellent for embroidery.

Rhinestones ❺

Rhinestones look like small precious stones with a flat back but are plastic. Use those with holes so you can sew them on firmly. Found in hobby shops.

Mosaic mirrors ❻

Mosaic mirrors are very small mirrors that can be either square or round. Use with shisha stitches (see pages 58–59).

Metal bells ❼

Small metal bells can be found in many shapes, colors and sizes. Use them as beads or for various styles of garland.

Ready-made appliqués ❽

Ready-made appliqués/fabrics can serve as effective details. They are often machine-embroidered and sometimes decorated with rhinestones and beads. Any good hobby or sewing shop should have them.

Decorative ribbons

Decorative textile ribbons can be either single color or patterned in different widths and qualities such as cotton and velvet and different art materials. You can use them for panels of embroidery, in the corners of a pillow or for the hanger on a tapestry. Good to have for something very simple. You can buy ribbon in handicraft stores, fabric and hobby shops or specialty ribbon shops.

For beads and mirrors, see photos overleaf

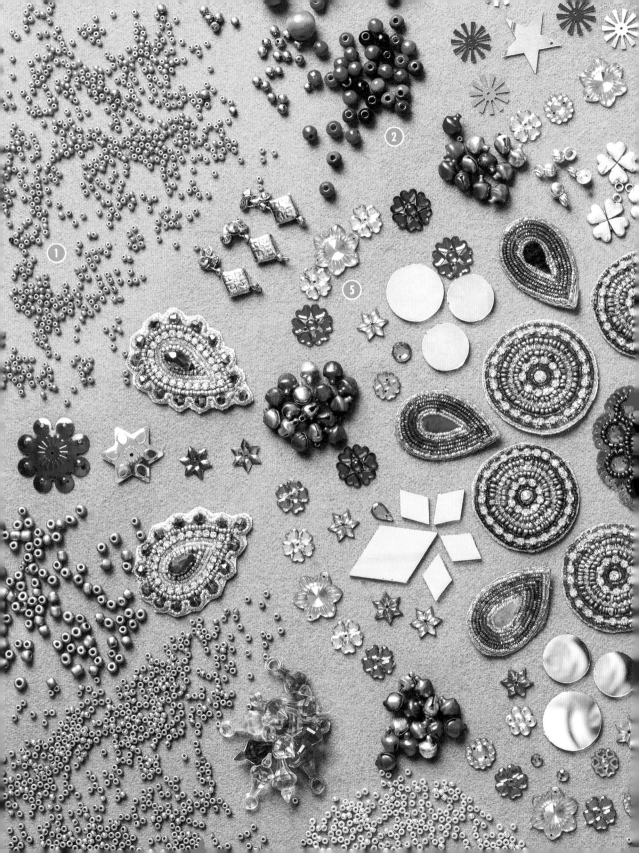

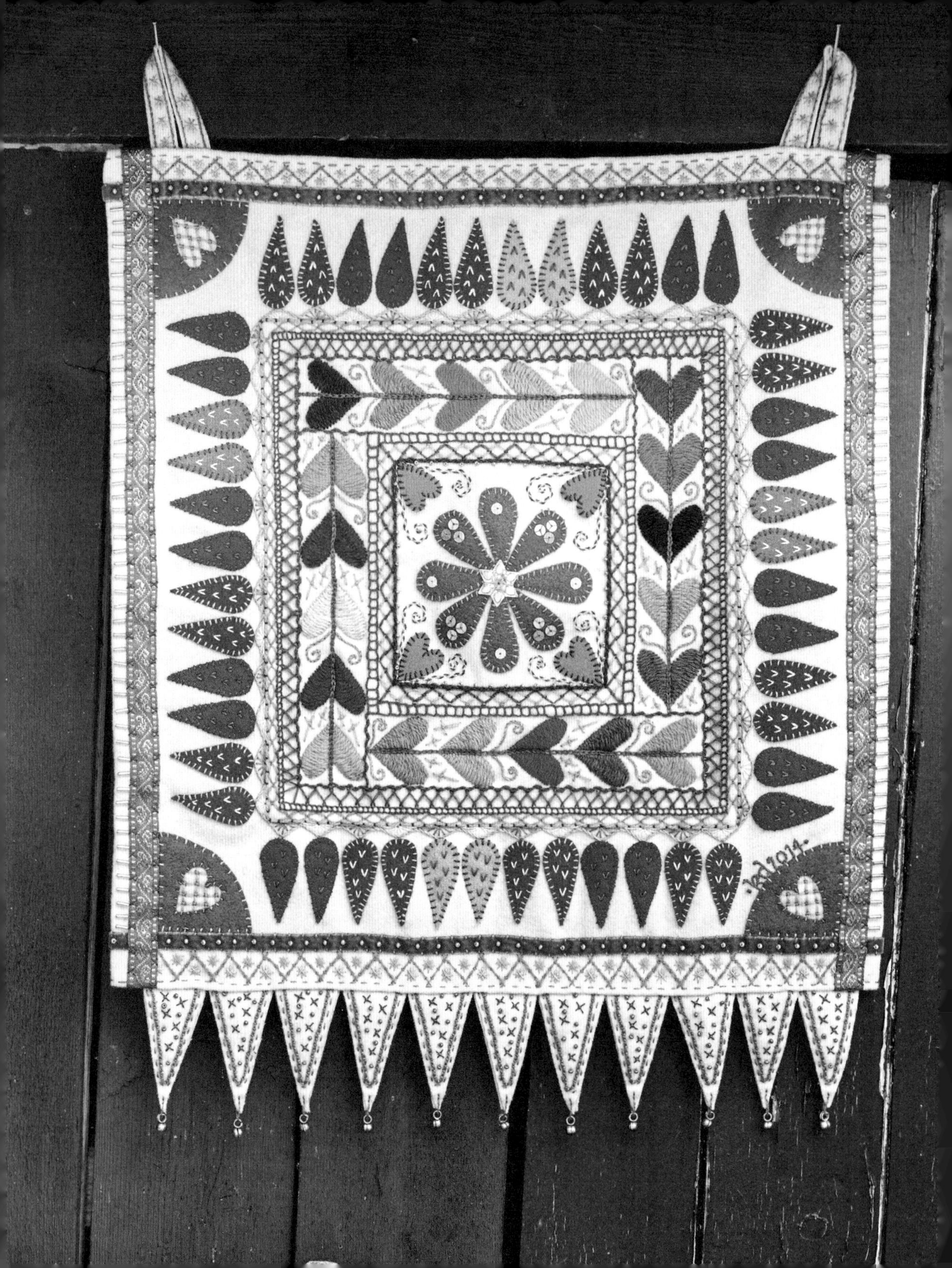
·kd2014·

Inspiration
– crystal clear or confusion

Everything that can be created by someone's hands is inspired by something. Every one is influenced by their surroundings. Places, meetings, people, architecture, bodies, animals, and plants, other art genres, abstract shapes, colors, feelings, thoughts, and psychological circumstances – everything we experience, see and absorb influences us and is expressed in what we create.

I am inspired by all kinds of things, including what I've listed here. I have always had a certain fascination for repeating patterns of various sorts. To pick apart the underlying shapes, which might be simple on their own, but together build something completely different, is interesting. I think constantly in pictures and shapes and often build my compositions successively like the overlapping waters of a stream.

TIP

Use your cell phone when you see things on the go, tear out pictures of patterns and shapes when you leaf through magazines. Save postcards and patterned pieces of fabric in a box or pin them to a wall.

TO BE INSPIRED BY SOMETHING SHOULD NOT BE CONFUSED WITH PLAGIARISM. Inspiration comes from seeing something that generates multiple ideas which eventually lead to your own, different, creation. You engage with an idea and then build on it but, although the result might have certain similarities to the original object of inspiration, it is obviously distinct. Something that has been plagiarized is a copy – either direct or almost. It can be constructive to copy solely to understand a process but the result can be uninspiring and it can be illegal if you want to show the work publicly.

FROM INSPIRATION TO EXPRESSION

PHOTO OF AN
INTERESTING BUILDING

A SKETCH OF THE INSPIRATION
SOURCE

FIND YOUR OWN
EXPRESSION – HERE THE
ARCHED WINDOWS
BECOME ONION-SHAPED.

SHAPES DRAWN ON CARDSTOCK,
THEN TRANSFERRED TO
APPLIQUÉ AND STITCHED
DIRECTLY ONTO FABRIC.

For some, the process of inspiration is crystal clear, for others it feels mixed. Will it be too abstract? Don't worry. Pictures, shapes, patterns and compositions can be found all over – on clothing, rugs, posters, buildings, in nature. The list can be endless. Take the time to look at different types of ornaments, mandalas, symbols, and graphics. Google, look in newspapers and books, pick up something you are automatically drawn to and go from there. In Sweden as well as in many other places in the world, you'll find rich embroidery traditions with distinctive styles and expressions – discover them. This is how you begin to see, looking and processing the impressions, and letting your own ideas take shape.

Here are some examples: Perhaps a detail on an old 1970s rug can be repeated to build a large edging panel to frame a central motif. Maybe the form of a flower on a piece of printed fabric can be stylized, enlarged, and become the center of a composition. Perhaps you are drawn to geometric or abstract shapes? Focus on that and experiment. Or, begin at the opposite end – develop an embroidery starting with a particular stitch technique and mix it with appliqué. Perhaps you like a certain landscape piece and its aesthetic – interpret it. Start from a patterned ribbon – what colors and shapes does it have? Let the ribbon set the tone by enhancing it with yarn, fabric and other materials.

If the result is not what you had envisaged

When you've gotten underway and suddenly realize "it is not actually all that good," you can always rip it out and re-do it. Some people think you shouldn't discard a piece you don't like, but you certainly can! One tip, however, whether you want to re-do the embroidery or just want to throw it away, try and resist. Either you can continue on the same piece by adding new details and stitches or you can set it aside and work on something else for a while. Sometimes on returning to it after a break you find you are okay with the stitches you previously hated.

GATHERING INSPIRATION

Patterns and shapes are everywhere. On other embroideries and fabrics, in architecture and embellishments of various sorts, in nature and on clothing, to list just a few!

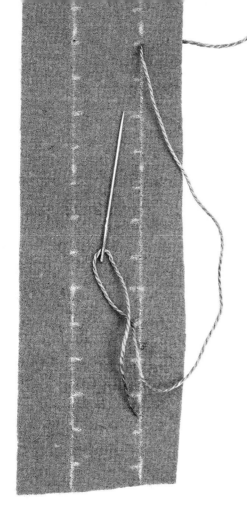

How do you begin?

Sometimes it can be hard to get going. "What should I do?" "Which colors work well?" "What should the embroidery look like when it's finished?" "What if it doesn't turn out well?" A long string of questions that only lead to, in the worst case, you sitting around without having made even a single stitch. You just have to begin. Before you begin, there is nothing to work with and there is nothing to change if you find other ideas along the way.

When I begin an embroidery, usually I have only decided what it should be, for example, a picture, a tapestry, or a cover. I might have a vague idea about the composition but never a detailed sketch or pattern that shows the final result. I begin with basic shapes and then build the embroidery after that. The embroidery is never a mechanically finished product of something decided ahead of time, but, an item to develop. Various parts and details are added and the embroidery moves successively through a sort of layer-on-layer principle where different materials and techniques – such as appliqués, ribbons, beads, and changing stitch types – are embedded.

A central component of this method is the usefulness of appliqué techniques in combination with stitches directly on the background fabric and on the appliqués. In a traditional landscape – or cross-stitch embroidery, for example, you fill in the surface only with stitches, often with only one or two types of stitches. In freestyle wool embroidery, you have endless stitch variations, appliqués, and other materials to help – many different modes can be blended.

A KNOT TO BEGIN WITH

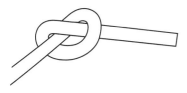

A simple overhand knot is the easiest one, although it is difficult to undo if you pull it too tightly.

IF YOU DON'T BEGIN THERE IS NOTHING TO WORK WITH AND THERE IS NOTHING TO CHANGE IF YOU HAVE OTHER IDEAS ALONG THE WAY.

DOES THAT SOUND DIFFICULT AND UNFOCUSED? HERE ARE A FEW TIPS TO GET YOU STARTED.

1. Think about what you want to make (perhaps a pillow cover, a hanging, or a cover for something).

2. Let's say you decide to make a pillow cover. What shape will it be? Square, rectangular, or maybe round? Should it be large or small?

3. Choose a color for the background fabric.

4. Begin composing a pattern by deciding on a shape to start from. Cut out one or more of the larger, basic appliqués and sew them on with whip stitch (see page 46) or buttonhole stitch (see page 47). If you want to add ribbons, sew them on the same way.

5. When the foundation is ready, you can continue with the somewhat larger details. Perhaps you want to embroider several appliqués or embroider several sections freehand directly on the fabric? Either sketch freehand, use the cardstock templates directly on the fabric, or transfer the desired pattern with pricking (see tips for pricking on page 39).

6. Now you can decide how to continue – you might begin with the finer details to edge the appliqués with laid work (see page 46) or stem stitch (see page 47) and beads. You can appliqué on top of appliqué (layer on layer) and then either embroider on them or sew beads on securely.

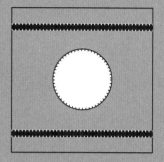

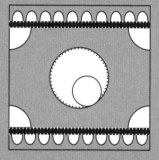

TIP

When working with several layers of appliqué, if you find the needle is getting stuck when, for example, sewing whip or stem stitch, just go down only into the nearest underlying layer of fabric.

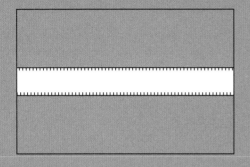

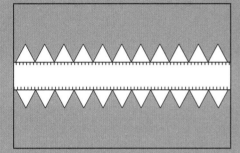

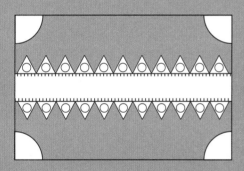

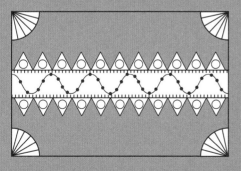

APPLIQUÉ TECHNIQUES

Begin with the bottom layer
– the larger shapes – when
appliquéing. Next, add the smaller
pieces, individual stitches and other
details. I never embellish a smaller
appliqué detail before I sew it onto
the embroidery. If I want to have a
circular appliqué form and fill it in
with French knots, I first sew down
the circle to the background fabric,
and then add the French knots. This
way, the work will be less fussy and
there is less chance of the small
appliqués fraying or losing their shape
– the final result will be much nicer.

FIND IT DIFFICULT TO DECIDE WHAT TO DO?

Make a sampler with a smaller
motif. You might make several
samples that you can join – instantly
you have the front of a pillow cover
or a wall hanging.

Creating a design

A design consists of shapes combined in a way to form a pattern. I usually gather my inspiration from traditional designs and what I see around me, but then develop them further and make my own patterns and combinations. I like symmetry and balance yet at the same time I love a multitude of elements, details, and a certain amount of irregularity, something that disturbs or interrupts the eye a little.

Of course, there are so many ways to consider embroidery and pattern compositions. My basic approach is to try and avoid too much detailed planning in advance, and instead, allow the embroidery to develop as I work. No matter whether you plan much beforehand or do it as you work, it's worth to considering a few simple ideas when it comes to basic composition:

• **Begin from the center.** Create a lavish center as the eye-catching feature and make the edges/sides more toned down (**A**). Focus on a central motif or shape. (**B**) and (**C**) are examples of compositions that can be viewed equally from all four directions, there really is no top or bottom.

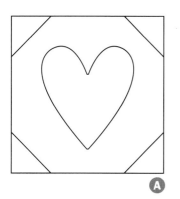

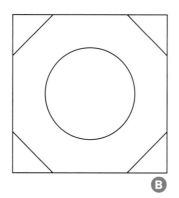

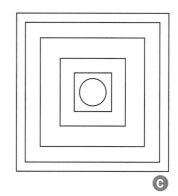

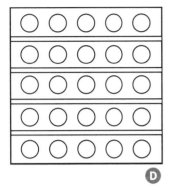

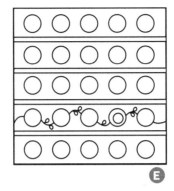

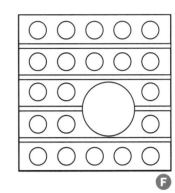

- **Aligned repetition** (**D**) – for example, repeating a panel pattern several times (creating stripes), alternating similar forms all over. There is no obvious center here and the composition is even but undynamic. To create something to disturb the eye, disrupt the patterning (**E** or **F**).

- **Mirror-imaging** If you are seeking harmony and balance but still want to produce a composition with an obvious top and bottom, an easy way to achieve the effect is to use reverse-imaging but only vertically. The top and bottom corners mirror-image each other respectively (**G**).

- **Framing** Move in the opposite direction and focus on producing a detailed and splendid outer edge. Tone down the center section (**H**).

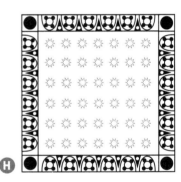

- **Shifting the central design away from the center of the piece.** An intentional lack of symmetry creates another dynamic (**I**).

One advantage of composing your embroidery as you go is that, if the whole feels a little disjointed, you only have to add more details. For example, fill out the sections with too much open space or where it feels a little too spread out. Because you don't have a set goal, there is no right or wrong and you shouldn't abandon something original. Keep going with what you feel is fine and good. When you always embroider in this way you will train your eye with regard to composition and stitch techniques as much as color.

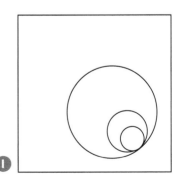

EXPERIMENT WITH A FEW SHAPES.

DUPLICATE, SHRINK, ENLARGE, AND
CREATE A VARIETY OF COMBINATIONS.

IDEAS USUALLY COME QUICKLY.

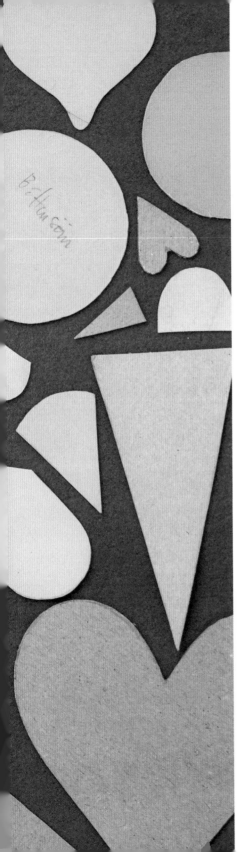

Easy templates

I usually work with cardstock and cardboard templates that I save and re-use. I sort them out into various boxes – one for circles, one for leaves, one for edged shapes, and so on. If I need a new shape, I can make it. My collection continues to grow.

How to make templates

When I need a particular shape, usually I begin by drawing it onto regular white paper or graph paper and cut it out. Then I lay the shape on the embroidery (fabric) and try it out to see if it works well or needs to be modified. When I am satisfied, I transfer the shape to thin cardboard or cardstock – it's more durable and makes it easier to draw the outline onto fabric. If you don't have sheets of thin cardboard or cardstock, try a cereal carton or some other food carton. They are sturdy and, at the same time, flexible enough to cut.

Three ways to use cardstock templates

• Draw the shape directly onto the background fabric and fill it with stitches, beads, etc.

• Draw the shape on a contrasting fabric, cut it out and then embroider it on as an appliqué to the background fabric.

• Draw the shape onto a larger appliqué. Cut the shape away so you have a reverse effect: a space.

Other ways to transfer the shapes to fabric

You can trace a shape or a pattern from one source and transfer it to the fabric with a pricking, or, draw freehand directly onto the fabric. I usually use all these techniques, depending on what works best in the particular circumstances.

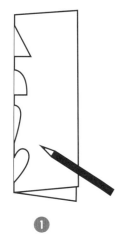

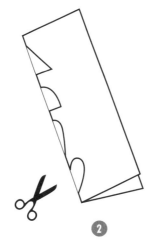

AN EASY WAY TO ARRANGE SYMMETRICAL SHAPES IN CARDSTOCK

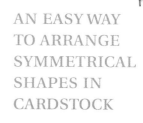

HOW TO ADJUST THE SHAPES TO FIT AROUND EACH OTHER

Lay the circle on the triangle and draw in the curve.

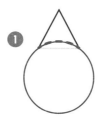

Cut away the marked area.

Ready!

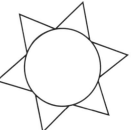

THE PRICKING METHOD

A flexible way to transfer a smaller pattern or shape to fabric is to trace it on with a plastic stencil with a water-resistant marker pen. Use a large needle to prick along the lines to make holes. Now lay the plastic template on the fabric and prick in all the holes again with a white or black marking pen.

TIP ●- - - - - - - - - - - - - - -

Draw freehand, trace the shapes from pictures or draw the contours. For circles, you can draw around a coin, glass, or other round object.

A few words
about color

Responses to and associations with different colors are very individual. Most people certainly have one or two favorite colors, I certainly do. Some colors are almost always included in a corner of my embroideries, others are very seldom seen, and some are never included. Differentiate between colors and shades (similar variations of a color). A broad color palette makes a diverse impression. Using only a few colors but in different shades produces a calmer and less overwhelming or busy impression. I start with a limited number of colors and reflect them in fabric, yarns and other materials. I then add different shades of the respective colors to create a deep and dynamic effect.

Try to do something different and use colors you normally might not choose; try out your favorite color in new variations and combination; begin with a color but use several shades of it.

Do you need color inspiration? Look around at your surroundings. Similar shapes and patterns can be found all around so you can scout out color combinations from existing objects. Experiment with yarns in different colors, lay them beside each other or set them in a "bouquet," take out one and add another – see what happens. That way, you can arrive at new combinations at the same time as you practice your color visualizations. Sometimes chance plays a role. Maybe you suddenly see something in the cord on the work table and, at the same time, catch sight of some yarn skeins that are serendipitously jumbled together. And voilà – a super color combo!

Two basic colors interact.

A moderated, harmonic impression with four very similar shades against a light background.

With a few details in pink, the effect deepens somewhat.

Against a dark background, the effect becomes totally different.

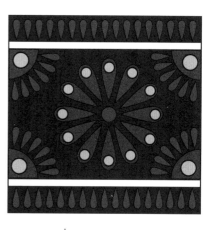

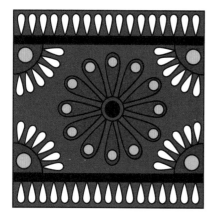

The same colors but combined differently.

The use of many colors automatically creates a busy effect.

The exact same color combination but with white stripes and a black background.

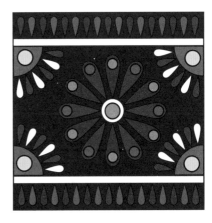

The darkest shades substituted with the two warm accent colors.

The red background and black leaves, rather than red, provide contrast with the background fabric.

As the previous example but with a dark background for a totally different look.

LOOK AND LEARN

Basic stitches, challenging stitches, and suggestions

for how they can be combined and used;

plus appliqué techniques and embroidery close-up.

Basic stitches

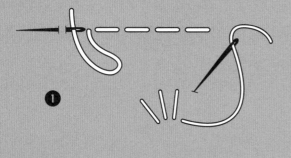

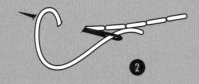

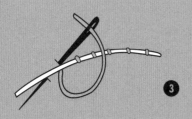

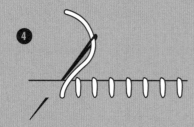

Running stitch

The needle goes up and down through the fabric with a small space between each stitch. Can be worked as individual straight stitches.

Good for: Lines and contours

Back stitch

Insert needle down behind the stitch and come up again the same distance in front of it. Each stitch directly follows the previous stitch – no spacing.

Good for: Lines, contours, and edging appliqué

Laidwork

Lay or stretch a thread/cord/string against the fabric and secure with a finer thread that encircles the cord before the needle goes down into the fabric.

Good for: Edging appliqués. For various types of panel, e.g to secure a heavy cord, thread, or string. Can be used to fill areas if laid closely together.

Whip stitch

Insert the needle diagonally through the lower layer so that the stitch is diagonal on the underside.

Good for: Sewing down appliqué, ribbons and much more.

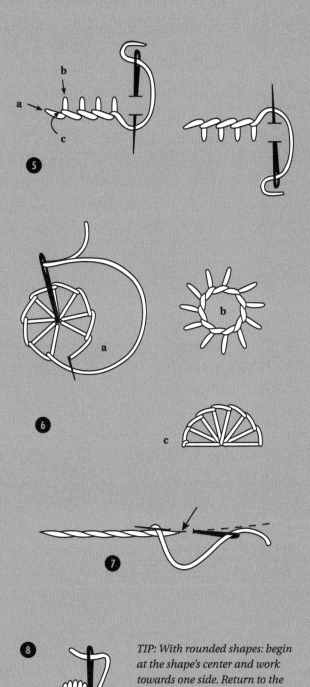

Blanket stitch

Bring needle up at **a**, down at **b**, and up again at **c** so stitches interlock. Can also be worked mirror-image so the vertical part of the stitch points upwards eg. as an edging around an appliqué.

Good for: Lines and borders and to attach or edge appliqué

Blanket stitch wheel

a) The same principle as in 5 with the needle always going down into the same place in the center of the circle.
b) The stitch pushes outwards.
c) Can also be worked in a half-circle.

Good for: Details

Stem stitch ⑦

For a cord-like look. Can be stitched in several ways; here, the needle comes up on the line about halfway along right side of previous stitch. You can also come up where the previous stitch ends (see arrow). Experiment! Make sure the thread always stays on the same side of the needle.

Good for: Lines and contours and for edging appliqué

Double-sided satin stitch ⑧

TIP: With rounded shapes: begin at the shape's center and work towards one side. Return to the center and stitch towards the opposite side. This method usually produces a more even result.

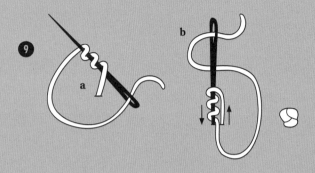

Double-sided satin stitch ⑧
(see illustration previous page)

Often sewn on from a sketched contour. The yarn follows the contour and the stitch looks the same on back and front of the fabric.

Good for: Filling in areas

French knot ⑨

a) Bring needle up through fabric, wrap the thread 3 times around needle depending the thickness of the thread and how large a knot you want. The needle tip should point upwards!

b) Insert needle down a tiny bit from original starting point. Pull the needle and thread through, making sure to hold the thread tightly as you work.

Good for: Most pieces – to edge appliqués and fill in areas and also as details. Use instead of beads – less likely to break. Provide a noticeable texture.

Herringbone ⑩

Begin at **a**, sew a diagonal stitch and go down at **b**. Come up again at **c** and down at **d**. TIP: Embroider between drawn lines.

Good for: Various kinds of border panels and to fill in areas. Vary with different colors, yarns, and by combining with other stitches.

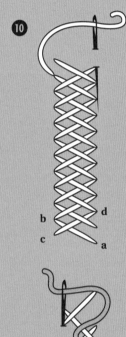

Mark small points where every downward insertion should occur, for example with ⅜inch/1cm space between each point.

Open
Increase the space between stitches.

Double
As shown, stitched with 2 colors. Sew one color and then the other.

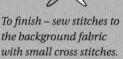

To finish – sew stitches to the background fabric with small cross stitches.

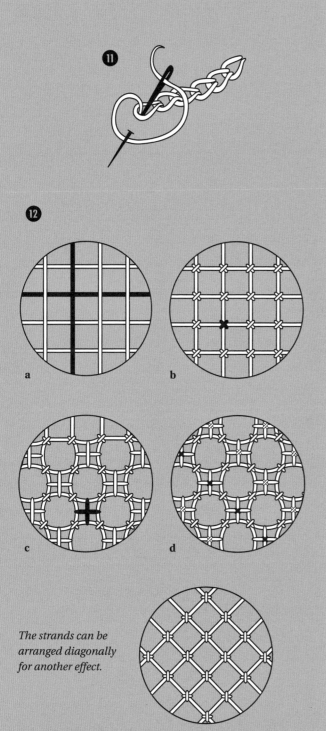

Chain stitch

Bring needle up and then down, always aligned. Don't pull the thread tight but leave enough to form a loop. Bring needle up again a bit further on, and make sure it comes up through the loop to create an interlocking chain.

Good for: Lines and to edge appliqué. Can cover areas if lines of chain sewn closely together.

Couching ⑫

Vary by arranging the strands in different ways and securing to the background fabric. I recommend using a hoop or frame, otherwise, the stitches can easily pull in together.

a) Spread the threads out horizontally and vertically to form a square. Begin by eyeballing or using a ruler; mark the fabric to ensure the threads are spaced evenly.

b) Secure the strands to the background fabric with small crosses. Leave as is or continue to steps c and d.

c) Embroider a cross over each block. The "holey" effect is produced by making the crosses somewhat smaller than the blocks they cross over.

d) Secure the crosses against the background fabric with mini-crosses.

Good for: Filling areas and shapes of various types

The strands can be arranged diagonally for another effect.

49

No. 1
"The Queen"

The heart is a universal symbol and here in green, was the starting point. Then the leaf shapes formed like fencing around it. After that, I wanted to frame everything to have a "skeleton" as a foundation. The little pod upon which the heart rests came about because it created an illusion of the heart floating. Once that was completed, I finished the bottom right corner. The left side is almost a mirror image of the right. A large embroidery such as this needs a regal framing so I experimented with various different borders. "The Queen" is mounted on a mitered frame (see page 133). The garland was last, after the embroidery was finished. It consists of metal bells, wooden beads and enamelwork such as were used on folk costume under bodices. The inspiration? Folk art splendor, Kurbits-style painting (see page 61), and organic forms.

Picture mounted on a frame
26½ x 21in/67 x 53cm

MATERIALS

Fine wadmal, mirrors, sequins, beads. Fine cotton fabric (lining)

THREAD

Wool, linen, flower and pearl cotton. Silk

STITCHES

Chain stitch, open chain stitch, whip stitch, running stitch, back stitch, stem stitch, blanket stitch, shisha, French knots, Mountmellick, herringbone, double-sided satin stitch, couching, laid work

Two-color chain stitch

This embroidery has an outer frame of two-color chain stitch (see above). This is sewn the same way as a regular chain stitch. The difference is that you thread two different colors onto the needle. Hold the color not in use above the needle. It will run alongside the other strand – but on the back.

1. Thread both colors onto the needle.

2. Make the chain stitches as usual with only one color forming the loop. Hold the color not in use above the needle.

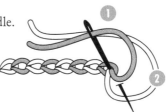

TIP ●- - - - - - - - - - -

Make a garland
The lower edge of the picture is finished with a garland of beads, bells, and jewelry components.

Appliqué over appliqué (wadmal) + rocaille beads

Open chain stitch (5/2 pearl cotton)

Double open herringbone secured with cross stitches and laid work (2-ply wool yarn + 16/2 linen thread + fine mercerized cotton)

Laid work (fine 2-ply wool yarn + 5/2 pearl cotton)

Threaded running stitch (Norwegian worsted yarn + 5/2 pearl cotton)

Crossed straight stitches (fine 1-ply wool yarn)

Double open herringbone secured with cross stitches (redgarn, doubled + redgarn, singles)

Stem stitch (5/2 pearl cotton))

French knots (redgarn, doubled)

TIP

See pages 92–97 for examples and descriptions of stitches and stitch combinations for various borders.

Laid work (tapestry wool + 16/2 linen thread)

Mountmellick, variation (5/2 pearl cotton)

Stem stitch (Brage yarn)

Double-sided satin stitch (tapestry wool, separated)

Appliqué (wadmal) with rocaille beads and details in 16/2 linen, Danish flower thread. Fine, matt cotton thread) and redgarn

Chain stitch (5/2 pearl cotton + 16/2 linen)

Appliqué (wadmal) edged with **chain stitch** (16/2 linen)

Double herringbone secured with cross stitches (Brage yarn + 5/2 pearl cotton)

Shisha (5/2 pearl cotton)

French knots (redgarn)

Herringbone (redgarn, doubled)

French knots
(16/2 linen) + rocaille beads

Double-sided satin stitch
(redgarn, doubled)

Double-sided satin stitch
(4-ply wool yarn, separated)

**Stem stitch and straight
stitch "twigs"** (silk)

French knots (5/2 pearl
cotton) + rocaille beads

Laid work (tapestry wool +
16/2 linen)

Double-sided satin stitch
(Brage yarn)

Whip stitch (5/2 pearl cotton)

Shisha (5/2 pearl cotton)

Straight stitch
(1-ply wool yarn, Fårö)

57

COMMON SHISHA

Consists of two main steps:
Foundation – the mirror is first attached to the background fabric. The edge – the mirror is then "dressed" with stitches that consolidate the foundation stitches.

Foundation

1. Attach the mirror to the background fabric by spanning the thread following figure 1. Spread the strands and make sure that the threads do not land too close to the edge of the mirror.

2. Secure by spanning threads diagonally.

The edge

3. Change to a new, rather long, strand (to avoid having to splice).
a) Bring needle up at arrow and draw through completely. Push the needle under the two foundation stitches holding the mirror.
b) Tighten slightly. If the foundation stitches from step 1 stretch out with the edge stitch to the edge of the mirror, they are not sufficiently taut.

4. a) Push needle down precisely where you brought it up on step 3. Do not pull through instead leave a little "loop" on the top side. **b)** Bring needle up again a few millimeters beside and through the loop, as for a chain stitch. **c)** Tighten.

5. Insert the needle under the foundation stitch and back out over the thread. Tighten slightly.

REGULAR

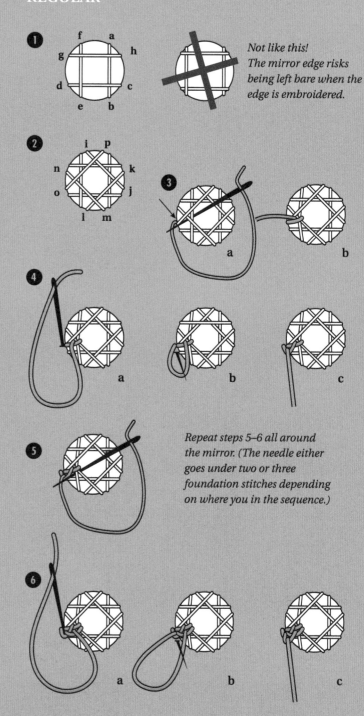

Not like this! The mirror edge risks being left bare when the edge is embroidered.

Repeat steps 5–6 all around the mirror. (The needle either goes under two or three foundation stitches depending on where you in the sequence.)

58

VARIATION

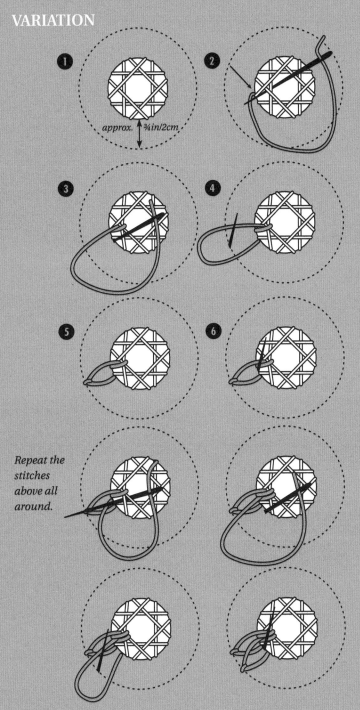

approx. ¾in/2cm

Repeat the
stitches
above all
around.

6. a) Insert the needle down into the previous chain stitch. **b)** Do not pull the whole strand through but make sure there is a little loop left to bring the needle up through so a new chain stitch can be made. **c)** Tighten slightly.

SHISHA VARIATION

Foundation

1. Attach the mirror as for a regular shisha. Draw a fine circle about ¾in/2cm larger in diameter than the mirror.

The edge

2. Change to a new, rather long, strand (to avoid splicing). Bring needle up at the arrow and draw thread through completely. Push needle under two foundation stitches attaching the mirror and over the thread you sewed with. Tighten slightly.

3. Insert needle down into edge of mirror and a couple of millimeters next to where the needle came up through the fabric. Do not pull all the thread through!

4. Bring needle up in the outer circle. Ensure a rounded loop is formed. Bring thread through completely.

5. Secure loop with a tiny stitch.

6. Again, bring needle up between the two previous downward stitches and draw thread through completely. Repeat steps 2–5 all around the mirror.

The stitches can be extended further (see page 62).

No. 2
"*Kurbits* Pumpkin"

This is a type of embroidered Kurbits or pumpkin painting (Kurbits is a style of painting popular from the late 1700s until the 1870s in Dalarna, Sweden). Exaggerated leaf and flower arrangements spring forth in a mixture of stitches, techniques and materials. The composition is worked from the center and the design reverses from side to side. It uses eleven different stitches.

Wall hanging
13½ x 16½in/34 x 42cm

MATERIALS
Fine wadmal, ribbon, beads, sequins. Fine cotton fabric (lining)

THREAD
Wool, linen, and pearl cotton. Silk

STITCHES
Whip stitch, stem stitch, back stitch, chain stitch, anklet stitch, mountmellick, shisha (variation), French knots, couching, laid work, herringbone stitch

Laid work (fine 2-ply wool yarn + 16/2 linen)

Blanket stitch (16/2 linen)

Closed Herringbone (tapestry wool, separated)

Open single chain stitch (redgarn)

Random straight stitches (16/2 linen)

EXTRA BANDS IN CONTRAST COLOR FOR SHISHA VARIATION

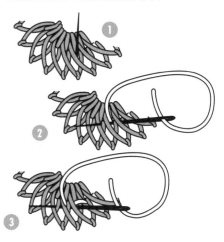

For the shisha variation described on page 59, you can add a contrast color.

1. Bring needle up.

2. Insert needle two strands to the right and then to the left under four strands. The needle does not penetrate the background fabric!

3. Repeat all around. End by inserting needle down through the background fabric where you began.

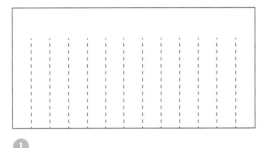

1

2

How to make the fringe

The fringe is embroidered in one piece and then cut apart and sewn on.

1. Cut a strip of wadmal or kläde. Measure and lightly draw placement of the fringes. Leave room at the top for later attachment.

2. Embroider all the fringes inside the markings.

3. Cut the fringe along the marked lines.

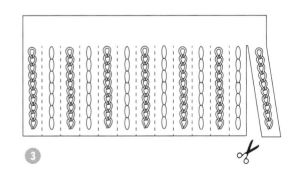

3

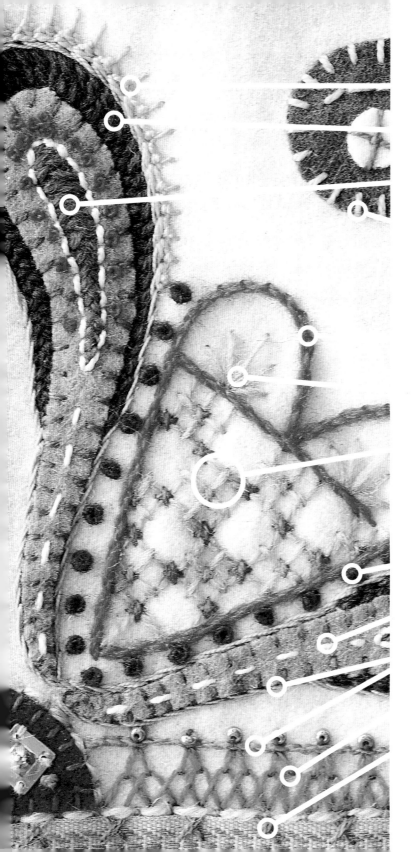

Mountmellick
(5/2 pearl cotton)

Closed herringbone
(tapestry wool)

Closed herringbone
(tapestry wool, separated)

Whip stitch
(5/2 pearl cotton 5)

Stem stitch
(2-ply wool yarn)

Straight stitch twigs
(1-ply wool yarn, Fårö)

Couching (2- and 1-ply
wool yarn + 16/2 linen)

French knots
(1-ply wool yarn, Fårö)

Running stitch
(1-ply wool yarn, Fårö)

Stem stitch (16/2 linen)

Anklet stitch
(Norwegian kamgarn)

**Ribbon attached with single
cross stitches** (redgarn, doubled)

No. 3
"Green Spades"

A wide, richly embellished horizontal band was my starting point here. I then added panels of stitches and ribbon. The triangular wadmal appliqués edging the central panel were only attached along the base, to add a fringed and somewhat fluttery effect.

Pillow
23¾ x 15¾in/60 x 40cm

MATERIALS
Fine wadmal. Recycled heavy cotton fabric for the backing. Various types of ribbons, pompoms for the corners

THREAD
Wool, linen, and pearl cotton

STITCHES
Whip stitch, running stitch, back stitch, stem stitch, blanket stitch, French knots, double-sided satin stitch, herringbone stitch

No. 4
"Pulp"

I started this piece with the border in Indian plaited stitch/sindhi. It is a rather advanced stitch requiring a great deal of patience and concentration. So, I shifted to the center section with couching. The composition is worked out from the center and has an obvious top and bottom. The flower buds are embroidered with pearl cotton and were inspired by Dala-Floda's påsöm embroidery tradition (Dala-Floda is a village in central Sweden). This embroidered piece has a very large number of beads and sequins, making it shimmer depending on where the light hits and the angle you look at it from.

Picture mounted on a frame
17 x 14½in/43 x 37cm

MATERIALS

Fine wadmal, mirrors, sequins, beads. Fine cotton fabric (lining)

THREAD

Wool, linen, and mercerized cotton yarn. Silk

STITCHES

Back stitch, whip stitch, stem stitch, chain stitch, and blanket stitch; Indian plaited/sindhi, shisha, mountmellick, French knots, couching, double-sided satin stitch

Indian plaited/sindhi stitch
(5/2 pearl cotton)

Outward-facing
blanket stitch (silk)

Blanket stitch (silk)

Threaded back stitch

The border around the embroidery is edged with the
Indian plaited /sindhi stitch (see page 97) with threaded
back stitch in green and pink.

1. Use color 1 for the
back stitch.

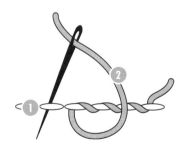

2. Change to color 2 and
wrap it around each back
stitch. The needle should
not penetrate the fabric.

Whip stitch (silk)

Shisha (5/2 pearl cotton)

Chain stitch (5/2 pearl cotton)

Blanket stitch (5/2 pearl cotton)

Back stitch (silk)

Threaded chain stitch (silk)

Double-sided satin stitch
(5/2 pearl cotton)

TIP

*Struggling to align the
edges of satin stitch?
If so, use another stitch,
such as stem, back, or
chain stitch to edge the
satin area and to hide
or fix any faults.*

Threaded back stitch
(Norwegian kamgarn + silk)

Couching (silk + 16/2 linen)

Herringbone (silk)

No. 5
Back cushion

The inspiration for this cushion comes from south Sweden. Skåne's wool embroidery is an embroidery tradition I haven't otherwise paid much attention to. After measuring and cutting out the black background fabric, I outlined five circles using a plate as a template. I improvised the design and drew freehand with a white gel pen. It has a mixture of various animals, flowers, leaf shapes, and flourishes. The broad color scale enhances the already rich overall look.

Back cushion
55¼ x 9¾in / 140 x 25cm

MATERIALS
Fine wadmal. Heavy furnishing fabric for backing. Ribbon for hanging. Wadmal tassels for the corners. Pillow insert

THREAD
Wool and linen yarn. Silk

STITCHES
Running stitch, back stitch, chain stitch, and stem stitch; blanket stitch wheel, French knots, double-sided satin stitch, long and short stitch

Appliqué techniques

Appliqué is the basis for this method of embroidery. The technique offers several modes of expression and increases the options for creating dimensionality in the embroidery, for both the surface and as a working technique. The interplay between the appliqué and the stitches worked directly onto the background fabric creates interesting structures. Wadmal is also ideal for cutting out shapes – it doesn't fray or tear. Here are a few tips to help you work with appliqué.

TIP
Never attach appliqué with fabric glue – it results in a hard surface that is difficult to embroider on.

1. For small appliqué pieces or appliqué with sharp corners, it is better to work downwards on the front of the appliqué than to go up from the back – this minimizes fraying.

2. With rows of similar appliqués, begin by securely sewing along the bottom. Then sew around all the contours in one go.

3. Draw the shapes on the back of the appliqué fabric (mirror-image if necessary) to avoid ink markings showing on the embroidery.

4. a) Reverse shapes, use a template to remove fabric on a larger appliqué to expose the background fabric.
b) Reverse shape, filled with another fabric.

5. When sewing several appliqués to each other with whip stich, on each layer the needle only needs to sew through the nearest underlying fabric.

6. The appliqué can be secured with small whip stitches in thread matching the fabric color and then "filled" with herringbone stitch.

7. A template made with a plastic stencil, see overleaf.

8. Here, a cardstock template was used to draw shapes directly onto the fabric. The shape is then filled with embroidery.

TRANSFERRING SHAPE DETAILS USING PLASTIC STENCILS

One advantage of outlining onto transparent plastic is that you can clearly see the on-going embroidery beneath it and try out different ideas before making a final decision. Step-by-step photos, left, show how to use a plastic stencil for testing various details/templates for both appliqués and shapes to be drawn directly onto the fabric. (See also page 39 for several examples of transferring with a plastic stencil.)

1. The space between the leaf shapes drawn with a marker onto plastic.

2. The shape is cut out and then transferred and transformed to a wadmal appliqué.

3. Reverse appliqué technique (a circle is cut out from the appliqué and filled with couching).

4. The plastic stencil used to sample details on the green appliqué. The shapes were drawn with a black marker.

5. "The leaves" cut out and transferred to cardstock (a firmer type of template).

6. The cardstock templates outlined with white Gelly Roll pen. Now it is ready to be embroidered (here double-sided satin stitch).

TRANSFERRING SHAPE DETAILS WITH CARDSTOCK TEMPLATES

Cardstock templates are firm and flexible. Step-by-step photos, right, show how to use cardstock templates for both appliqués and embroidering directly onto the fabric. (For more about templates and appliqué techniques, see pages 37 and 76.)

1. Cardstock in the desired leaf shape. Placed on the background fabric so you can draw around it.

2. Two cardstock templates (the same shape but different sizes) are used and traced directly onto the background fabric. A third, even smaller piece, a pink appliqué, is sewn down securely with whip stitch.

3. The outer contours are filled in with double-sided satin stitch.

4. Prepare design for further details on the pink appliqué. Use templates to draw shapes directly onto the fabric.

5. The details from step 4 are embroidered on with double-sided satin stitch. More appliqués are cut out, ready to be sewn on.

6. The whole piece is now completely embroidered.

No. 6
"Lotus"

When I began this embroidery, all I had decided was
that it would be a large hanging "tapestry". My first
step was drawing the center circle and cutting out the
appliqué pieces for the blue leaves in the center. Then the
embroidery grew bit by bit out from the leaf shapes and
their color. I experimented quite a lot with various stitches.
The composition is geometric with various "borders" that
build on each other. The leaf/teardrop shapes were inspired
by Indian embroideries. The flowers in the corners derive
from motifs found in *påsöm* embroidery from Dala-Floda
in the Dalarna region of Sweden.

Hanging "tapestry"
24 x 28in/61 × 71cm

MATERIALS
Fine wadmal, beads, sequins, ribbon,
mirrors, appliqué. Fine cotton fabric
(lining for back)

THREAD
Wool, linen, flower, and pearl cotton. Silk

STITCHES
Open chain stitch, stem stitch, blanket
stitch, whip stitch, anklet stitch, French
knots, shisha, double-sided satin stitch,
couching, herringbone stitch, spider web
filling stitch

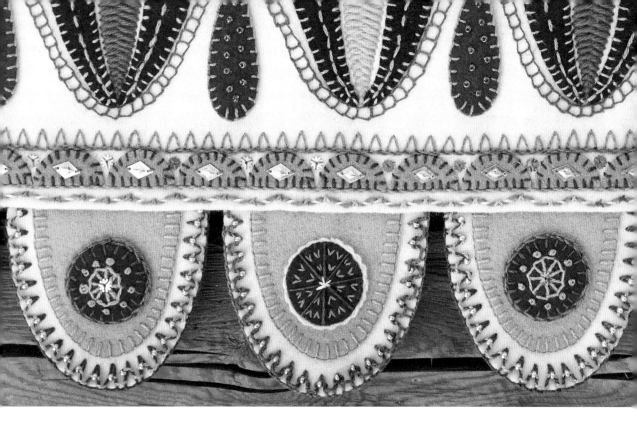

Blanket stitch variation for edgings

The "fringe" above is edged with a type of blanket stitch.
After stitching it, I overlaid it with a strand strung with beads.

1. Begin by bringing the thread up from the back.
Make a diagonal blanket stitch.

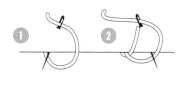

2. Make another diagonal stitch, leaning in the opposite
direction to form a triangle.

3. Continue the same way ending by securing the final
eyelet on the back of the piece.

4. Thread another strand around the blanket stitches
(see above). Using a bead needle string the beads and thread
through the diagonal blanket stitch strands as shown.

5. End by fastening off on the back.

Blanket stitch wheel
(16/2 linen)

Couching (tapestry wool
+ 16/2 linen)

Single open chain stitch
(16/2 linen)

Straight stitch "fans"
(16/2 linen)

Stem stitch (redgarn, doubled)

Laid work (heavy 2-ply wool
yarn + 5/2 pearl cotton)

Reverse appliqué technique
(see pages 76–77)

Couching (wool yarn,
Zephyr + 16/2 linen)

Anklet stitch (5/2 pearl cotton)

Stem stitch (Brage yarn)

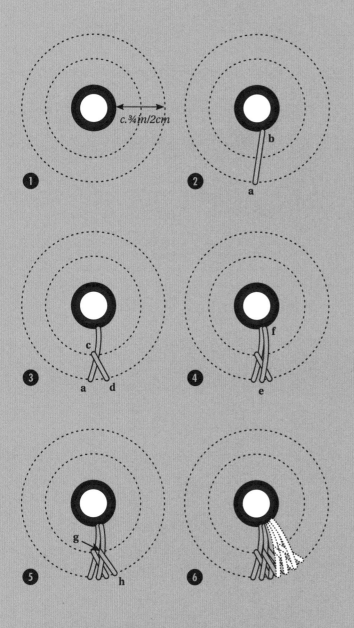

(commonly found in Indian embroidery)

The **shisha stitch** (see pages 58–59) is common in Indian embroidery. Sometimes it is edged by a type of herringbone stitch that I call a shisha moon.

1. Embroider a regular shisha. Draw two circles around the embroidered mirror – a larger circle and a smaller one, with the radius of the larger one about ¾in/2cm out from the edge of the shisha.

2. Bring the needle up at **a** and make a long, slightly diagonal, stitch to **b** at the edge of the shisha.

3. Bring the needle up at **c** and make a little stitch down to **d** (about ¼in/5mm from **a** in the previous step).

4. Bring the needle up at **e** and down at **f**.

5. Bring needle up at **g** (that is, at the line of the smaller circle and between the long stitches). Needle goes down at **h**.

6. Continue the same way all around.

NOTE: *The white and black center sections correspond to a mirror plus shisha stitching (see page 58). In other words, the mirror plus the small stitches at the center of the picture on the page opposite.*

No. 7
"Leksand"

As the title suggests, much of the inspiration for this embroidery came from the Leksand folk costume (Leksand is a town in the Dalarna region of central Sweden). I was very taken with the swirly shapes worked in herringbone embellishing the women's bodice and the shoulders of the men's costumes. For the shisha stitching on the stars, I experimented with origami paper on cardstock rather than mirrors. The ribbon is considered a Leksand ribbon. The pompoms at the bottom edge resemble the knee decorations of the man's costume.

Picture mounted on a frame
17¾ x 17¾in/45 x 45cm

MATERIALS
Wool furnishing fabric (background fabric), fine wadmal (appliqué), paper, cardstock, beads, ribbon. Fine cotton fabric (lining)

THREAD
Wool and pearl cotton. Silk

STITCHES
Stem stitch, whip stitch, shisha, couching, herringbone

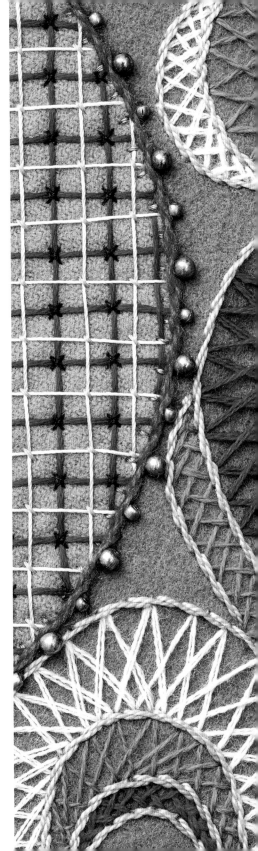

HOW TO MAKE POMPOMS

You can make the **pompoms** with the classic method, using circles of cardboard with a hole in the center or with a plastic pompom maker so you don't have to cut out new cardboard templates for each new pompom. It's fast work filling up a pompom maker with yarn – you wrap one half at a time so you don't have to bother with a tapestry needle around an ever tighter hole

TIP

Shisha without mirrors
For shisha embroidery, you might try substituting a piece of fine paper or pretty fabric glued to sturdy cardstock (see right) for the mirror.

Border stitches

Some stitches are particularly good for borders, edgings and finishing. Some are excellent just by themselves but you can create complex patterns by combining different stitches which are otherwise quite simple. Here are a few examples with descriptions, both for single stitch variations and stitch combinations that can be used for frames, borders, and edgings. I've developed some of the combinations by experimentation. Once you begin, the possibilities are endless. NOTE: Several of the combinations include basic stitches. They are marked with an asterisk (*) and are described in detail on pages 46–49.

Mountmellick **1**

Half blanket stitch wheel* **2**

Back stitch* **3**

Anklet stitch **4**

Laid work* **5**

Threaded running stitch **6**

Open chain stitch **7**

Combination of herringbone*, French knots,* chain stitch,* and back stitch* **8**

Straight stitch twigs* **9**

Combination of straight stitch* and stem stitch* **10**

Combination of running stitch* and single chain stitch* **11**

Combination of open herringbone/laid work* and stars **12**

Blanket stitch* + diagonal blanket stitch (see page 84) and French knots* **13**

Couching* **14** edged with laid work*

Indian plaited stitch/ sindhi **15**

Straight stitch cones* **16**

See overleaf for stitched examples

❶ Mountmellick

1. Bring needle up at **a** and make a diagonal stitch ending at **b**. Bring needle up again at **c** – directly below **b** and aligned with **a**.

2. Twist the thread under the diagonal stitch by pushing the needle underneath it from left to right.

3. Push needle down at **a** again. Leaving a loop of thread.

4. Bring needle up through the loop just formed (exactly as for a chain stitch).

5. Draw thread through completely and continue immediately to the next stitch going down at **b**.

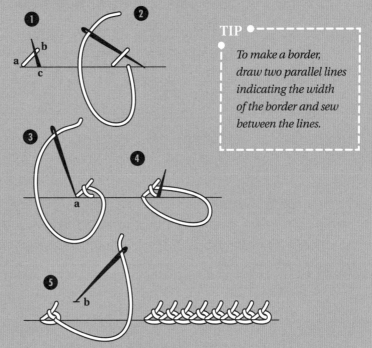

TIP ●--------

To make a border, draw two parallel lines indicating the width of the border and sew between the lines.

❹ Anklet stitch

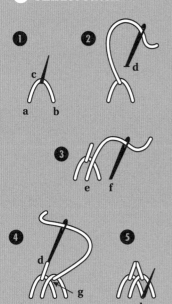

1. Bring needle up at **a** and down at **b** – don't draw thread completely through before once again bringing needle up at **c**, to create a loop.

2. Go down at **d** and draw thread through completely.

3. Bring needle up at **e** – in the center of the first loop and then down at **f**. Don't draw thread through completely.

4. Bring needle up at **g** and end at **d**.

5. Begin next stitch at **b**.

❻ Threaded running stitch

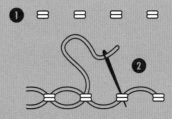

1. Stitch pairs of running stitch spaced equally apart along the line to be embroidered.

2. With another thread, work up and down through the running stitches to form loops. The needle only loops through the stitches and does not go through the fabric.

93

TIP

*Do you have trouble
making a neat turn at the
corner? Use a variation of
the stitch or cover the
corner with appliqué.*

7 Open chain stitch

1. Bring needle up at **a** and then down at **b**, angle the needle diagonally and come up again at **c**. Make sure the thread stays under needle.

2. Insert needle at **d**, continue forming linked loops.

TIP: You can change the look of this stitch by varying the spacing of the loops.

11 Running stitch and single chain stitches

1. Make a regular chain stitch.
2. …. but secure the loop with a small stitch.

1. Single chain stitch
2. Running stitch
3. Back stitch

8 Herringbone, French knots, chain stitch, and back stitch

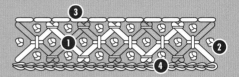

1. Herringbone secured with cross stitch plus running stitch at top and bottom.

2. French knots
3. Back stitch
4. Chain stitch

9 Twigs of straight stitch

Sew the long center stitch first, to set the size for the remaining branches.

10 Running stitch and stem stitch

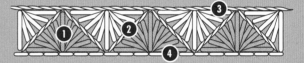

1. Running stitch
2. Stem stitch
3. Stem stitch
4. Back stitch

Draw 2 parallel lines and then draw the triangles between the lines before you begin the embroidery.

12 Open herringbone/laid work and stars

. **1.** Open herringbone secured with laid work

2. Straight stitch stars
3. Back stitch

15 Indian plaited/sindhi stitch; also called double herringbone

This stitch consists of two steps. First, a foundation is sewn with two turned herringbone stitches. Then another thread is woven in. NOTE: Study the diagram carefully to see how the foundation strands loop over/under each other. This is essential so that the braiding in step 2 can work.

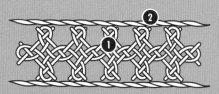

1. Indian plaited/sindhi stitch
2. Stem stitch

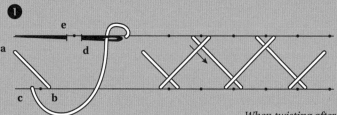

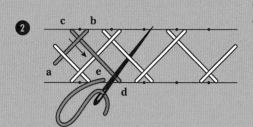

When twisting after **e** *in step 1 and again after* **c** *in step 2 – make sure that the needle moves* **under** *the crossing strands (see arrow).*

Herringbone

1. Draw two parallel guide lines. Measure to ensure that the lines are parallel and also make small marks where the needle will go down. This method helps produce more even results.

Begin by bringing the needle up at **a**, down at **b**, up at **c**, down at **d**, and up at **e**.

Continue to embroider the open herringbone the same way all along the line.

2. Embroider another turned open herringbone (drawn in gray here to make it easier to see how the threads intersect) to form a double herringbone line.

Weaving in

3. Begin at **a** and let needle loop through the lattice following the diagram. Alternate the needle going over and under the crossed strands.

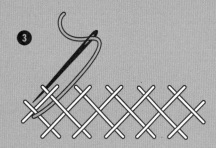

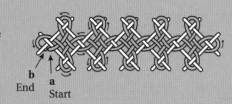

b
End

a
Start

16 Straight stitch cones

Make the center stitch first to set the size.

No. 8
"Green lotus"

The original inspiration for this hanging, a personal favorite, is a patterned woven band with a green background and red hearts that my grandmother gave me long ago. I had this and the lotus flower in mind from the beginning. I like the color combination, the lotus shape, and the linen laid work which lies so nicely and fills in the space above the red ribbon. The pennant pairs constituting the scalloped fringe at the bottom are embroidered with couching. Otherwise, it is the only time – so far – that I have used brown wadmal.

Hanging
11 x 14½in/28 x 37cm

MATERIALS
Fine wadmal, ribbon, beads, sequins. Cotton fabric (lining)

THREAD
Wool, linen, and flower thread

STITCHES
Running stitch, back stitch, stem stitch, whip stitch, French knots, couching, laid work

No. 9
"Toran 1"

A toran is a common type of hanging in India that
has always fascinated me. They are placed in door
openings as a way of welcoming the gods and people
into the house, and are often elaborately decorated
with flowers and symbols. The toran pictured here is
my first full-sized one and consists of a joyful mixture
of classic påsöm flowers, Indian shisha embroidery
and a lot of herringbone. Because I like couching,
I wanted to test making some in a large format.
This resulted in the whole embroidery resting on a
background of herringbone worked in silk. "Toran 1"
was embroidered in a frame I made myself (see page
130) because I didn't have anything suitable on hand.

Hanging
34¾ x 20½in/88 x 52cm

MATERIALS
Fine wadmal, sequins, beads, mirrors,
jewelry components, rhinestones.
Fine cotton fabric (lining)

THREAD
Wool, linen, and pearl cotton. Silk

STITCHES
Back stitch, running stitch, whip
stitch, stem stitch, chain stitch, blanket
stitch (var.), shisha, French knots,
couching, double-sided satin stitch,
herringbone, laid work

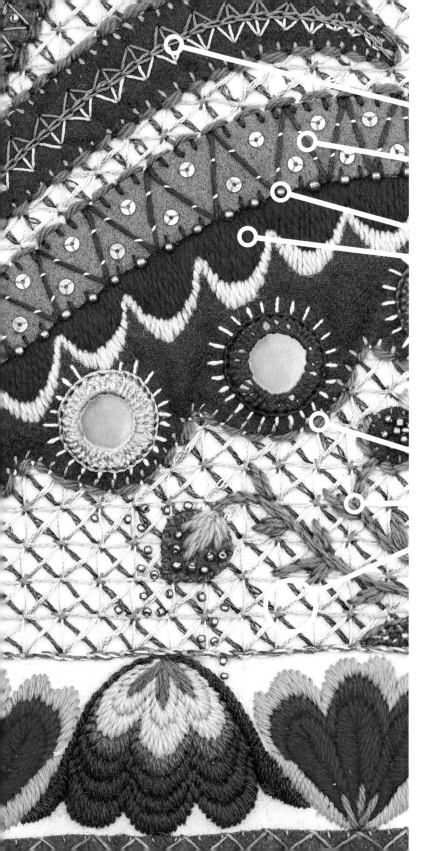

Chain stitch and straight stitch "cones" (silk)

Open herringbone secured with laid work (16/2 linen, doubled + fine mercerized cotton)

Round metal beads

Double-sided satin stitch (Tuna yarn)

Laid work (tapestry wool + 16/2 linen)

Stem stitch (tapestry wool)

Couching (silk + 16/2 linen)

TIP

Appliqué is more impressive if it is edged and embroidered so that, overall, it appears more fully worked.

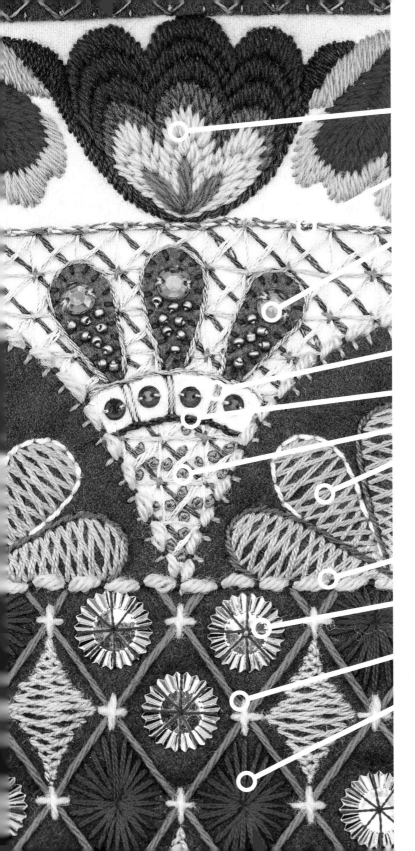

Double-sided satin stitch
(tapestry wool, separated)

Laid work with hand-twisted
cord (silk and mouliné metallic
+ 16/2 linen)

Rhinestones and **rocaille beads**

Double running stitch (silk)

Stem stitch (5/2 pearl cotton)

French knots (silk)

Herringbone (silk, doubled)

Laid work (tapestry wool
+ 16/2 linen)

Large sequins attached with
redgarn

Couching (4-ply wool yarn +
Tuna yarn)

Straight stitch stars
(silk, doubled)

3

EMBROIDERY PROJECTS

Step-by-step instructions for an armband, decorative case, hanging medallions, and pillow cover. Plus how to construct an embroidery frame, wet-blocking embroidery, and finishing your work.

Armband

MATERIALS

- Fine wadmal
- Narrow decorative ribbon
- 5/2 pearl cotton or a
similar thread you have on
hand and want to use
- Rep (warp-faced) band
for lining
- Waxed lace thread or
strong sewing thread
- Hooks and eyes

How to make

1. Find a piece of woven rep band the same width the armband will be. Decide on the length of the armband by measuring the wrist circumference and adding 1–1½in/ 3–4cm.

2. Cut a piece of wadmal, the length and width of the armband measurements (for example, 1½ x 8in/4 x 20cm).

3. Measure the width of the decorative ribbons and save some space for them at each side. Draw two parallel lines at the center of the armband. Embroider Indian plaited/ sindhi stitch between the lines (see page 97).

4. Sew on the decorative ribbons (with small whip stitches and fine thread) along the edges of the sindhi stitching, not along the outer edges. If you want, embroider stem stitch in the space between the herringbone and the ribbon and securely sew on beads.

5. Fold in the ends of the armband (about ¾in/2cm on each side), pin and then sew on hooks on one short side and the eyes on the other.

6. Pin the rep band to the back of the armband and, with back stitch and waxed lace thread, seam the whole armband from the right side along the decorative ribbons' outer edges and the short side.

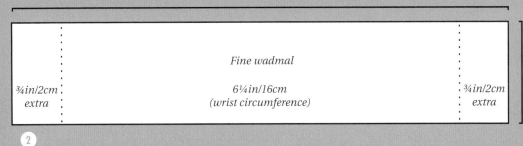

8in/20cm (example)

1½in/4cm (example)

Fine wadmal

6¼in/16cm
(wrist circumference)

¾in/2cm
extra

¾in/2cm
extra

2

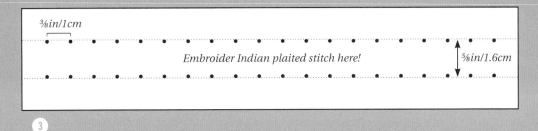

⅜in/1cm

Embroider Indian plaited stitch here!

⅝in/1.6cm

3

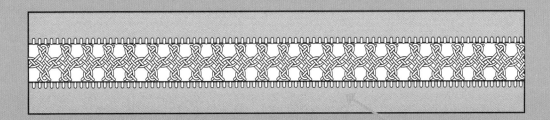

4

Only attach the
ribbon along the
herringbone edge.

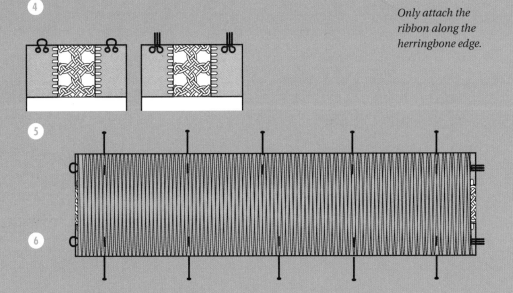

5

6

Rep band

Alternate closure with a
waxed cotton loop and
button instead of hooks.

**Indian plaited/
sindhi** (Brage yarn)

**Stem
stitch**
(16/2
linen)

**Indian plaited/
sindhi**
(3/2 pearl
cotton)

Rocaille beads
metallic, sewn on
with waxed lace
thread.

SIZING SUGGESTIONS

This **pattern** makes an armband 1½in/4cm wide and approx. 6¼in/16cm long when finished. You can adjust the length of the armband to fit your own measurements; the width is determined by the width of the rep band.

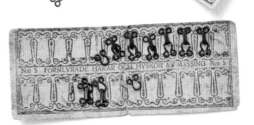

DO YOU HAVE A SPOOL OF STRONG THREAD?

Use it instead of waxed lace thread for sewing on the band.

Decorative case

MATERIALS

- 2 pieces wadmal or similar (6¼ x 8¼in/16 x 21cm)
- Patterned ribbon (width: ⅝in/1.5cm length: 8¼in/21cm)
- Thread: 5/2 and 8/2 pearl cotton, medium weight wool yarn, tapestry wool, 16/2 linen, lace
- or sewing thread – or similar.
- 5 round mirrors (diameter: ¾in/18mm)
- Rocaille beads
- Zipper (6in/15cm)
- Cotton lining fabric

If you want to know exactly which threads were used, see annotation on pages 116–117.

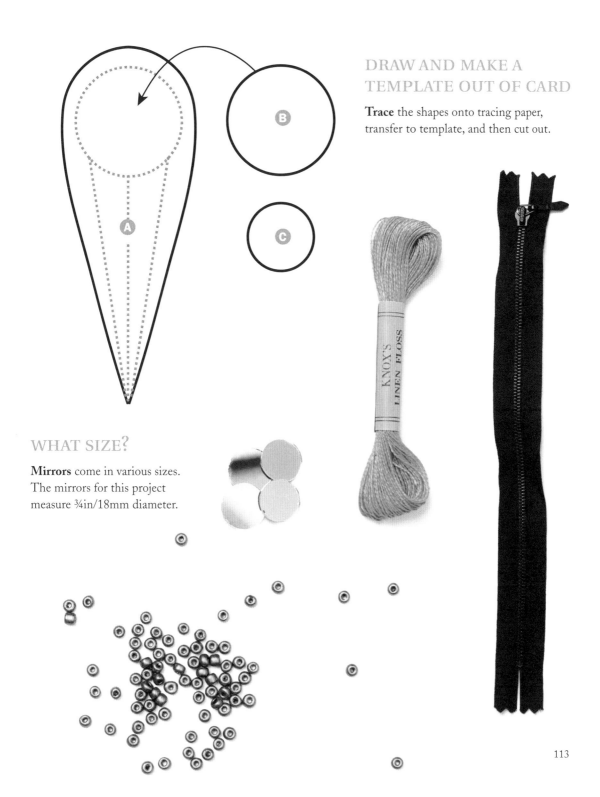

DRAW AND MAKE A TEMPLATE OUT OF CARD

Trace the shapes onto tracing paper, transfer to template, and then cut out.

WHAT SIZE?

Mirrors come in various sizes. The mirrors for this project measure ¾in/18mm diameter.

1

Begin by sewing on the ribbon.

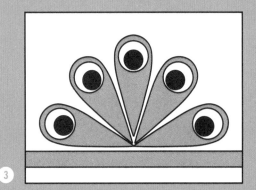

Leave small gaps between the appliqués and above the ribbon

2

Cut out all the appliqués A. Arrange them on the background fabric, making sure there is a ¹⁄₁₆–¹⁄₈in/2–3mm gap between each and above the ribbon to leave space for the laid work to be added later.

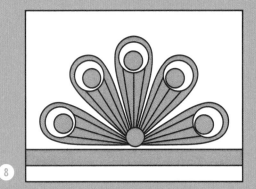

3

Sew on the mirrors with shisha stitch.

5

Draw three lines on each appliqué and embroider lines with back stitch.

8

Cut out appliqué C and sew it down so it covers the tips of appliqué A.

TIP

If it feels awkward to hold the mirrors still while you attach them with shisha, secure each with a drop of textile glue, allow to dry before sewing down.

How to make

1. Pin and then sew the ribbon on with small whip stitches, about ⅝in/1.5cm from the lower edge.

2. Cut out the appliqués (5 pieces, template A). Use small, sharp embroidery scissors to cut out a circle at the tip of each appliqué (using template B). Arrange and pin down the appliqué pieces on the background fabric and sew down securely with small whip stitches.

3. Place the mirrors at the bottom of each appliqué circle and sew down with shisha stitch. (If it makes it easier, attach each mirror with a drop of textile glue before sewing it down.)

4. Embroider French knots in the remaining space of each circle (see overleaf).

5. Draw three lines from the tip to the edge of each circle and back stitch along each line.

6. Sew beads around each circle (see overleaf).

7. Edge each appliqué A and the top side of ribbon with laid work (see overleaf).

8. Cut out appliqué C and sew down with small whip stitches. Next, sew a doubled cross of straight stitches and attach it with a single cross stitch in the center. Sew on the beads and edge with laid work (see detail overleaf).

9. Work French knots around the three center "leaves" and edge bottom of ribbon with chain stitch.

10. Wet block the embroidery and leave until dry (see page 131). Line, sew in zipper and then sew down lining by hand or machine.

Lining: It is a good idea to line covers, cases or bags, if only to protect the back of the embroidery. If you can't manage to sew on a complete lining and fold it in, you can, instead, face the embroidery by sewing a protective lining fabric to the back of the embroidery. I usually use a zigzag stitch on the machine.

Zipper: There are various ways to sew in a zipper. I usually sew this type of case on the machine, leaving an opening for the zipper which I then sew in by hand with running stitch.

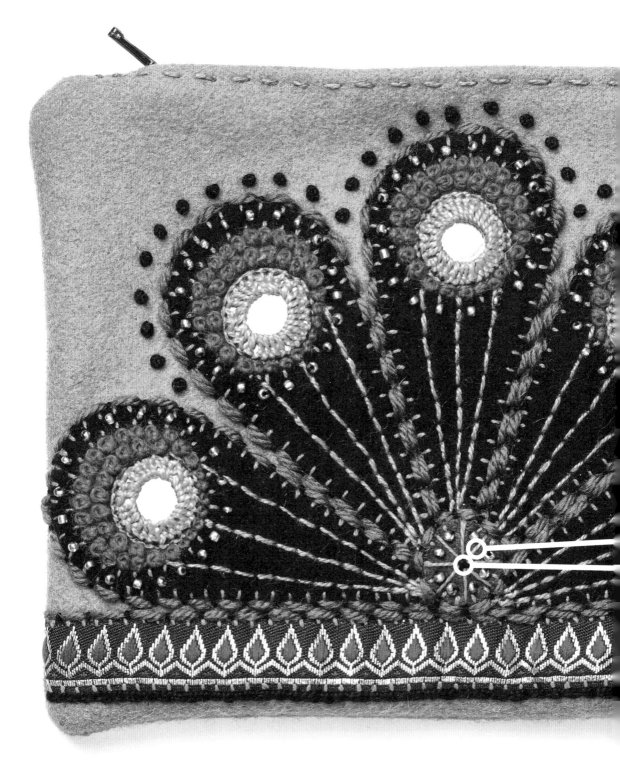

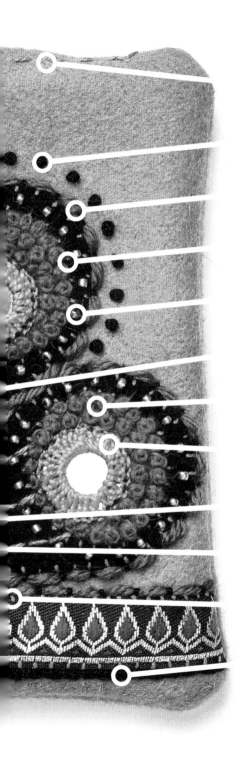

Zipper sewn in with **running stitch** (16/2 linen)

French knots (5/2 pearl cotton)

Laid work (tapestry wool + 5/2 pearl cotton)

Whip stitch (8/2 pearl cotton)

Beads (lace thread)

Back stitch (16/2 linen)

French knots (medium weight 6/2 wool yarn)

Shisha (5/2 pearl cotton)

Doubled cross of straight stitches (8/2 pearl cotton)

Single cross stitch (5/2 pearl cotton)

Whip stitch (8/2 pearl cotton)

Chain stitch (5/2 pearl cotton)

Hanging Medallions

Do you want to know precisely which thread was used? See details on pages 122–123.

MATERIALS
- Wadmal (approx. 11¾ x 11¾in/ 30 x 30cm)
- Thread: silk, pearl cotton, lace or sewing thread (for beads) – or other threads you have to hand
- Rocaille beads (large and small), mirrors, small bells
- Fine steel thread (type for jewelry making)
- Cardboard (*c.* ¹⁄₃₂ in/1mm thick)

Embroider inside the dotted line.

B

A

DRAW AND MAKE CARDSTOCK TEMPLATES

Trace the shapes onto tracing paper, transfer to cardstock, and then cut out.

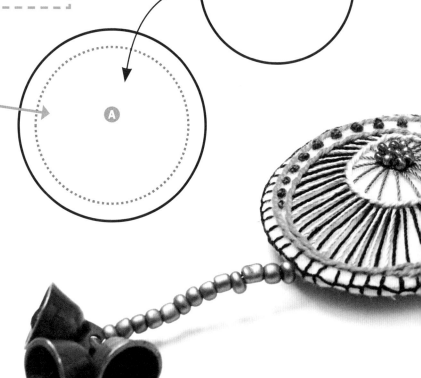

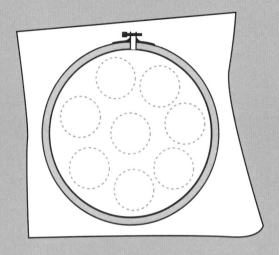

1 Stretch the fabric and draw the circles.

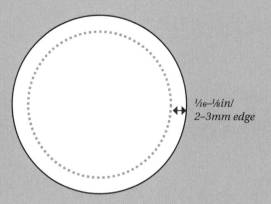

$\frac{1}{16}-\frac{1}{8}in/$
2–3mm edge

2 Leave a small space (a few millimeters) around each circle for the blanket stitch.

3 To stabilize the piece, wedge a piece of cardstock inbetween the embroidered circles.

4 Sew the circles in pairs using blanket stitch all around.

TIP •----------------------------

Because the medallions can turn and both sides will be visible, watch carefully where the needle comes out on each side when joining the circles. Otherwise, the stitches may shift and the edge will be even only on one side.

How to make

1. Stretch the fabric in an embroidery hoop (about 8¼in/21cm in diameter or larger). Using template A, draw an even number of circles.

2. Embroider each circle as you like. Experiment with mirrors and/or other elements that gleam and capture the sunlight. Leave a small space around the edge so that you can later join the pairs of circles with blanket stitch around the edges. (Template B works well for drawing out appliqué A.)

3. After embroidering the circles, you can remove the fabric from the hoop and cut each one out. Arrange them in pairs with wrong sides facing. To stabilize each piece, wedge in a smaller piece of cardstock between the embroidered circles before joining them.

4. Join the circle pairs using blanket stitch around the edges.

Finishing

Attach some bells, a large bead, or similar to the bottom with steel thread. String various types of beads and wind through the medallions (it's easier to use a needle longer than the diameter of each circle). Form a hanging loop at the top.

INSTEAD OF A HANGING

These **circles** are useful for all sorts of things, such as keychains.

Blanket stitch (silk)

Blanket stitch (silk)

Stem stitch (silk)

Shisha (5/2 pearl cotton)

Double herringbone stitch
(5/2 pearl cotton + 16/2 linen)

Large rocaille beads
(3.6 x 3mm) + fine steel thread

Blanket stitch (silk)

French knots (16/2 linen)

Rocaille beads
(metallic + opaque)

Straight stitch (silk)

Stem stitch (5/2 pearl cotton)

Blanket stitch (silk)

Couching (silk)

Double herringbone stitch
(silk)

Rocaille beads (metallic)

Back stitch (silk)

Blanket stitch (silk)

Rocaille beads
(metallic + matt)

Shisha (5/2 pearl cotton)

Shisha moon (5/2 pearl cotton)

Back stitch (5/2 pearl cotton)

Pillow cover with decorative ribbon

MATERIALS

- Fine wadmal (18¼ x 18¼in/ 46 x 46cm for background fabric + extra for appliqué and loops)
- 1 wide decorative ribbon (W: 2in/5cm; L: 18¼in/46cm)
- 2 narrow ribbons (W: ⅝in/1.5cm; L: 18¼in/46cm)
- Rocaille beads
- Thread: 5/2 pearl cotton, 16/2 linen, wool yarn (var. sizes and qualities), fine cotton thread, lace thread – or other you have to hand
- Backing fabric
- Pillow insert 19¾ x 19¾in /50 x 50cm

Do you want to
know precisely which
thread was used?
See details on
pages 128–129.

Trace the shapes onto tracing paper,
transfer to cardstock, and then cut out.

F

B   D

E

C

*Draw the outlined shapes
freehand directly onto the fabric
or trace them and make
cardstock templates.*

A

How to make

1. Cut a piece of background fabric, 18¼ x 18¼in/ 46 x 46cm, including a ⅜in/1cm seam allowance.

2. Center section. Measure out the center of the background fabric. Pin the wide ribbon and attach with whip stitch.

3. Pin into place and then sew on the narrow ribbons leaving ¾in/2cm space on each side of the center ribbon.

4. Trace template A onto tracing paper, then transfer to cardstock; cut out (see page 125). Draw 28 "teeth" on fine wadmal and cut out. Sew them on with blanket stitch only along the base at the outer edges of the narrow ribbons.

5. Fill the empty spaces between the ribbons with embroidery. Begin with herringbone stitch and then continue with the details in it. End with stem stitch (see page 128).

6. Corners. Cut out appliqué B. Sew down securely edge to edge to the corners of the background fabric. Sew the curve with blanket stitch and the straight edges with running stitch (the latter won't show once the pillow cover is seamed). Cut out appliqués C and D. Place these about ⅜in/1cm in from the edge and sew down with small whip stitches. Cut out E and sew onto D.

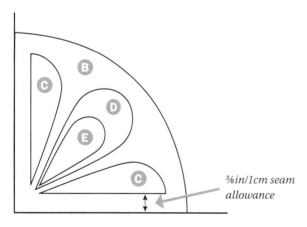

⅜in/1cm seam allowance

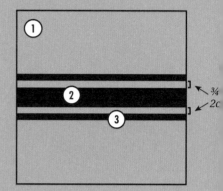

¾
2c

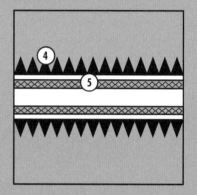

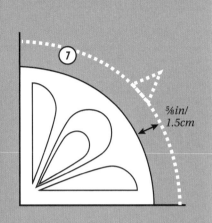

⅝in/
1.5cm

*The loops at the corners are made with two strips of fine wadmal. Sew **b** with small whip stitches to **a** and then embroider the remaining stitches.*

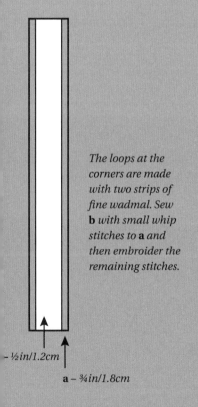

– ½in/1.2cm

a – ¾in/1.8cm

7. Draw a curve parallel to appliqué B, ⅝in/1.5cm outside it. Embroider the gap. Next, draw the "teeth" to edge the corner by transferring template F to cardstock and then tracing it directly onto the background fabric. Fill the shapes with embroidery, even embroidering the lines between the herringbone and teeth (see page 129 for stitches and threads).

8. Embroider the remaining details on the corners (see page 129 for stitch and thread suggestions). Repeat steps 6–8 on the other corners.

9. Finishing. Stretch the embroidery evenly, dampen, and leave until dry (see pages 131 and 134).

10. Cut out strips of fine wadmal for the corner loops. Embroider them (see page 129) and ease them into the corners as you join the front of the cover with the back (your choice of backing). I usually use waxed 16/2 linen thread or lace thread when I seam pillow covers. Use an invisible stitch to seam opening after inserting pillow form.

TIP

Corner loops: Outline four strips on the fabric and embroider before you cut them apart so there will be less fraying (the same principle as the fringe on page 64).

Blanket stitch (5/2 pearl cotton)

Threaded running stitch (16/2 linen)

Stem stitch (1-ply wool yarn, Fårö)

Whip stitch (fine cotton thread)

Open double herringbone secured with cross stitches (Klippan's wool yarn + 16/2 linen)

Stem stitch (Norwegian worsted – kamgarn, doubled)

Running stitch (16/2 linen)

Rocaille beads (gold)

French knots (5/2 pearl cotton)

French knots (Tuna wool yarn)

Straight stitch "twigs" (5/2 pearl cotton)

EXTRA DETAIL

On this pillow cover, I embroidered threaded running stitch on the narrow ribbons and running stitch along the contours of the center ribbon (see detail). You can always stitch along the design on your selected ribbon.

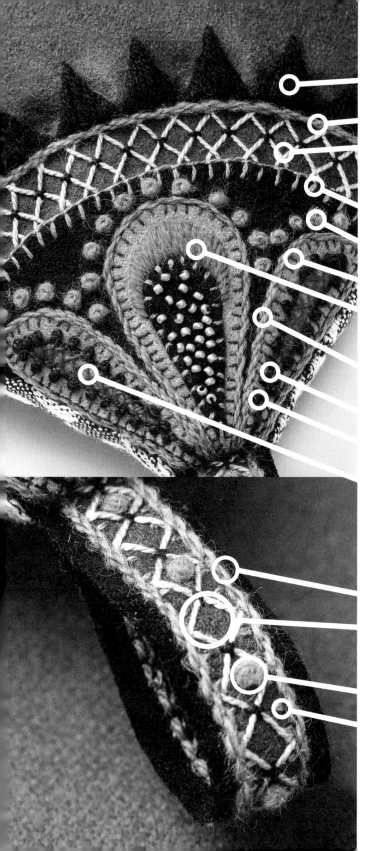

Double-sided satin stitch (redgarn)

Stem stitch (Klippan's wool yarn)

Open double herringbone secured with cross stitches (pearl cotton + 16/2 linen)

Blanket stitch (16/2 linen)

French knots (Tuna yarn)

Whip stitch (fine cotton thread)

Double-sided satin stitch (Norwegian worsted – kamgarn, doubled)

Stem stitch (Norwegian worsted – kamgarn, doubled)

Back stitch (5/2 pearl cotton)

French knots (5/2 pearl cotton)

Herringbone (16/2 linen)

Stem stitch (Klippan's wool yarn)

Open double herringbone secured with cross stitches (pearl cotton + 16/2 linen)

French knots (Tuna yarn)

Whip stitch (16/2 linen)

How to make an embroidery frame

Although not a necessity for making large embroideries with appliqué, a frame can make the job easier as the entire embroidery is stretched as you work. There are adjustable frames to buy but here's a model you can make to your preferred size. It is not adjustable but it's easy to make. You just need are four frame pieces, corner braces and a drill.

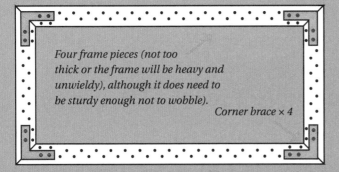

Four frame pieces (not too thick or the frame will be heavy and unwieldy), although it does need to be sturdy enough not to wobble).

Corner brace × 4

Drilled holes so that the background fabric can be attached with stretcher threads in the frame.

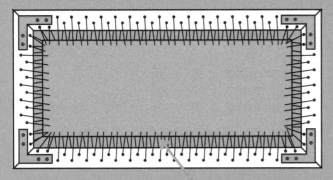

The fabric is attached to the frame with stretcher threads.

The pillow corners can be shaped in different ways.

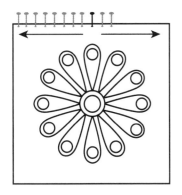

1 *Beginning at the center, pin towards the sides.*

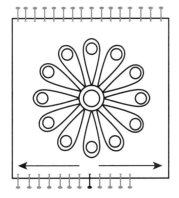

2 *Pin the opposite sides first.*

3 *Spray the embroidery with water.*

How to finish your work

When the embroidery is complete, it should be stretched with the right side facing up so that it will be nice and smooth. You can do the blocking yourself. It's the last step needed to ensure that, for example, a pillow cover or hanging is truly complete.

Wet blocking

Wet blocking is done when the embroidery is complete but before it is mounted. Block the piece by stretching it out on a soft wood fiber board covered with cotton fabric. A board covered with cotton fabric marked off in squares is useful for aligning the embroidery. I normally eyeball the position. There are several ways to wet block and what you choose depends on how much time you have. I don't do this but here are a few more tips:

• Pin out the piece quite tightly.

• Beginning at the center, pin out to the sides while making sure the embroidery is smooth and stretched – but not too tightly – or it might pucker at the edges.

• Pin out the opposite sides first.

• Spray water onto the embroidery so that it is damp but not wet. Leave it to dry – preferably overnight or longer.

Finishing the back of hangings

For pictures and hangings, I recommend that you protect the back of the embroidery. I normally use a fine cotton fabric and keep to a simple finishing. I cut out a lining the same size as the embroidery, fold in the edges on both lining and embroidery, place them with the wrong sides facing and then join them with small running stitch from the back. NOTE: The running stitch should not go through to the front of the embroidery, but only be sewn into the folded edge. Don't forget to miter the corners if you prefer that. If the piece is a picture mounted on a mitred frame, I fold the lining edges towards attached sides of the embroidery on the back of the frame and sew it down with small running stitches.

> TIP
>
> *Hanging loops can be decorative and enhance the embroidery. The examples to the right show several options.*

Mounting on a mitered frame

You'll need: four slats or stretchers for the frame, wedges, sheeting, staple gun, folding ruler/ruler, pen, scissors.

Begin by arranging the four slats of wood into a square. These are stabilized with small wedges of wood in the corners. Here are a few basic tips:

• **Join the frame pieces** – use a rubber hammer and a piece of fabric or something soft for protection so that the frame pieces won't be damaged as you join them.

MITERED FRAMES

Just like paintings, embroideries can be mounted on a mitered frame. You can buy this type of frame in an art supply shop or online. The stretcher pieces are sold individually and come in a range of lengths. Choose the lengths you need and then you can assemble a frame that fits your piece. NOTE: Leave a couple of inches/a few centimeters of the background fabric around the entire embroidery so you can stretch it around the frame.

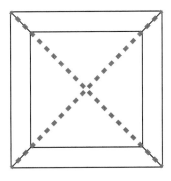

When the frame is joined: Measure it diagonally in both directions. A mitered frame that is properly squared at the corners should have exactly the same measurements corner to corner.

• **When the frame is assembled** – measure the diagonal carefully to make sure that the frame is straight with corners at right angles. It often looks straight but it rarely is and then you have to adjust by tapping lightly until it is.

• **Backing with sheeting** – to protect the embroidery from rubbing against the frame. First stretch sheeting or another type of fine cotton fabric on the frame. Attach it with a staple gun, beginning at the center and working out to the sides, while making sure that the sheeting is stretched taut. Always do the opposite sides first, leaving the corners for last. Corners are the most difficult part and you need to turn in the edges a bit differently at the corners. If you don't quite understand this step, check the internet for more detailed instructions.

• **After the frame** is covered by the cotton fabric, staple the embroidery on the same way, taking even more care.

• **With fine cotton fabric,** sew on a protective backing (see previous page). Finally, screw in the hanging loops or hooks if you want.

Assembling a pillow cover

Wet block the embroidery (see page 131) and let it dry completely. Cut out the backing the same size as the front. Zigzag stitch the edges if there is any danger of the fabric fraying. I normally use a heavier cotton fabric – often older fabrics I've found at flea markets and other such places – but sometimes even furnishing fabric. I often pick out some shapes – and color tones – from the front and reflect those elements in ribbons or appliqué on the back, sometimes with my signature.

Place the front and back with right sides facing, pin and then seam the pieces with a ⅜in/1cm seam allowance. Leave an opening about 8in/20cm on the lower edge of the cover. I usually seam pillow covers by hand with whip stitch and waxed linen, but, of course, you can use the sewing machine if you prefer.

Turn the cover right side out. Insert the pillow form and finish seaming with invisible stitching.

If you are adding pompoms, tassels, loops or something else which will protrude at the corners, you can poke the extra piece in and secure it as you seam the cover. Or, you might leave small openings at each corner and sew in the corner details last. Poke them in from the right side, fold in the edges, and again stitch by hand.

An invisible stitch makes an invisible join and so is good to use when you are sewing up the last seam of a pillow cover.

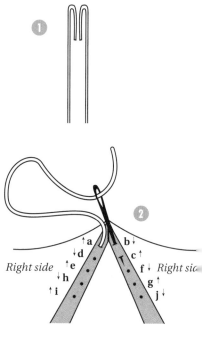

1. Fold in the hems on each side of the opening and place them edge to edge.

2. Begin at **a** and then stitch alternately into the folded hem edges. Do not pull the edges in too close together or the fabric will crease and the seams buckle.

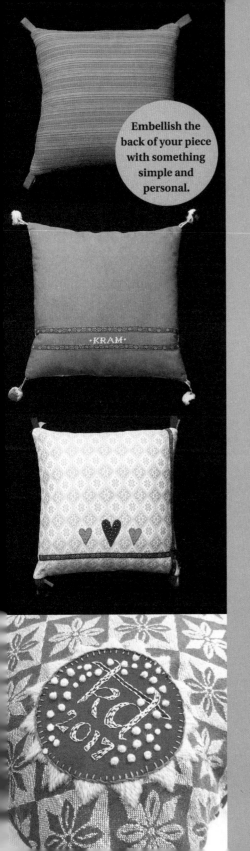

Resources

If you live outside Sweden, you can order the materials listed in the book from these shops. You can also visit many of them – the addresses are listed on their respective websites.

• Brodera Mera, *www.broderamera.se* – wadmal, threads, notions, tools, etc.

• CCHobby, *www.cchobby.se* – beads, mirrors, and loads of other materials!

• Harry Hedgren, *www.harryhedgren.se* – wadmal, kläde, etc.

• Hemslöjd (Swedish handcraft) shops
Hemslöjden Skåne, www.hemslojdenskane.se
Svensk hemslöjd, www.svenskhemslojd.com
Sätergläntan, www.cronacraft.se
(for more shops, see www.hemslojden.org) – threads, yarn, wadmal, kläde, books, notions, tools, etc.

• Kilramar.se, *www.kilramar.se* – mitered frames, mounting tips, inspiration, etc.

• Kreatima/Panduro, *www.panduro.com* – mitered frames, pens, paper, etc.

• Skapamer, *www.skapamer.se* – beads, mirrors, and much more!

• Slöjddetaljer, *www.slojd-detaljer.se*
– beads, jewelry components, tools, and a large assortment of other materials.

• The Historical Fabric Store, *www.thehistoricalfabricstore.com*
– wadmal and kläde.

• For the Swedish yarns (Brage, Fårö, Mora redgarn, Tuna) listed in this book, see *store.vavstuga.com* (Vävstuga Weaving School in Massachusetts).

And don't forget flea markets and small sewing shops located where you might least expect them. Plus all the bead, yarn, ribbon and fabric stores you can find when abroad.

Notes

ACKNOWLEDGEMENTS

Ulla Parkdal, textile artist – for everything. How can I ever return the favors?

Helene Hombert Qvist, gallery owner of Roddarhuset in Vaxholm – for encouragement, wisdom, and your strong belief in me and my work.

Katarina Klingspor Ekelund, artist – because you saw and said that my work must be out in front of the camera.

Ninni Ahlsell, artist and decorative painter – for your encouragement and tips, and because you turn up a little haphazardly in my life. You are fierce!

Jenny Unnegård, photographer – because you made me laugh and for your unique eye. This book is equally yours.

Cecilia Ljungström and Ulrika Rapp, Hemslöjdens förlag – It was so wonderful to make this book with you. I am honored.

Jenny Berge, Managing Director, Svensk Hemslöjd – for all your prodding, pep talks, fingertip sensitivity, and, not least, your sharp eyes when it came to the instructions – you are a rock!

Varemet and Possumbroderi (Instagram) – for hangings, threads, encouragement and for going outside the box.

Family, friends, Instagram followers and everyone who goes their own way – you are so inspiring!